ALCOHOL-FREE COCKTAILS

REDEMPTION BAR

ANDREA WATERS + CATHERINE SALWAY

Andrea and Catherine are the brains behind Redemption, one of London's healthiest bar restaurant brands serving up sugar-free, wheat-free vegan dishes with an alcohol-free bar. Catherine has a background in marketing with extensive media experience, while Andrea is a successful chef and entrepeneur with a passion for nutrition.

KYLE BOOKS

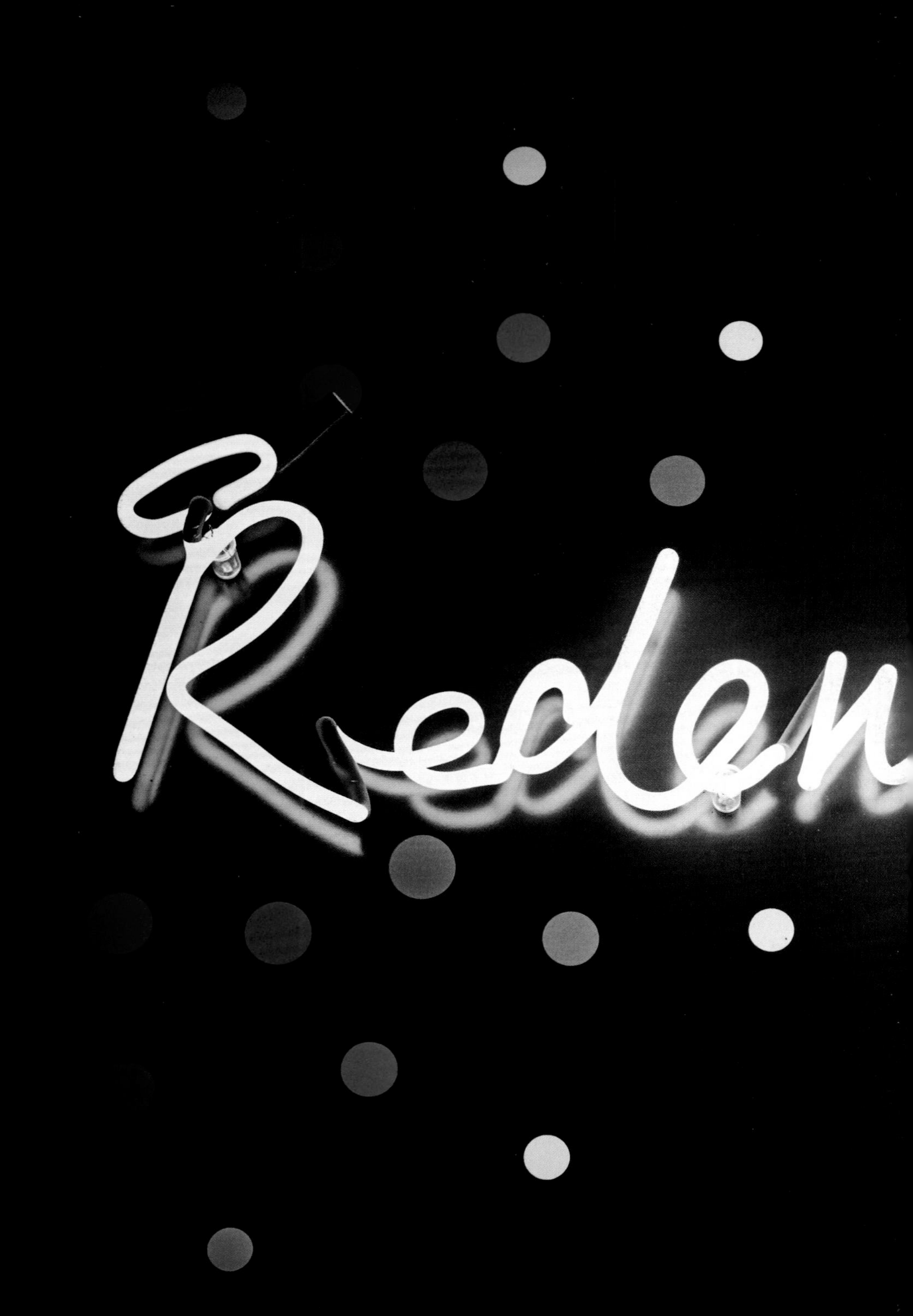

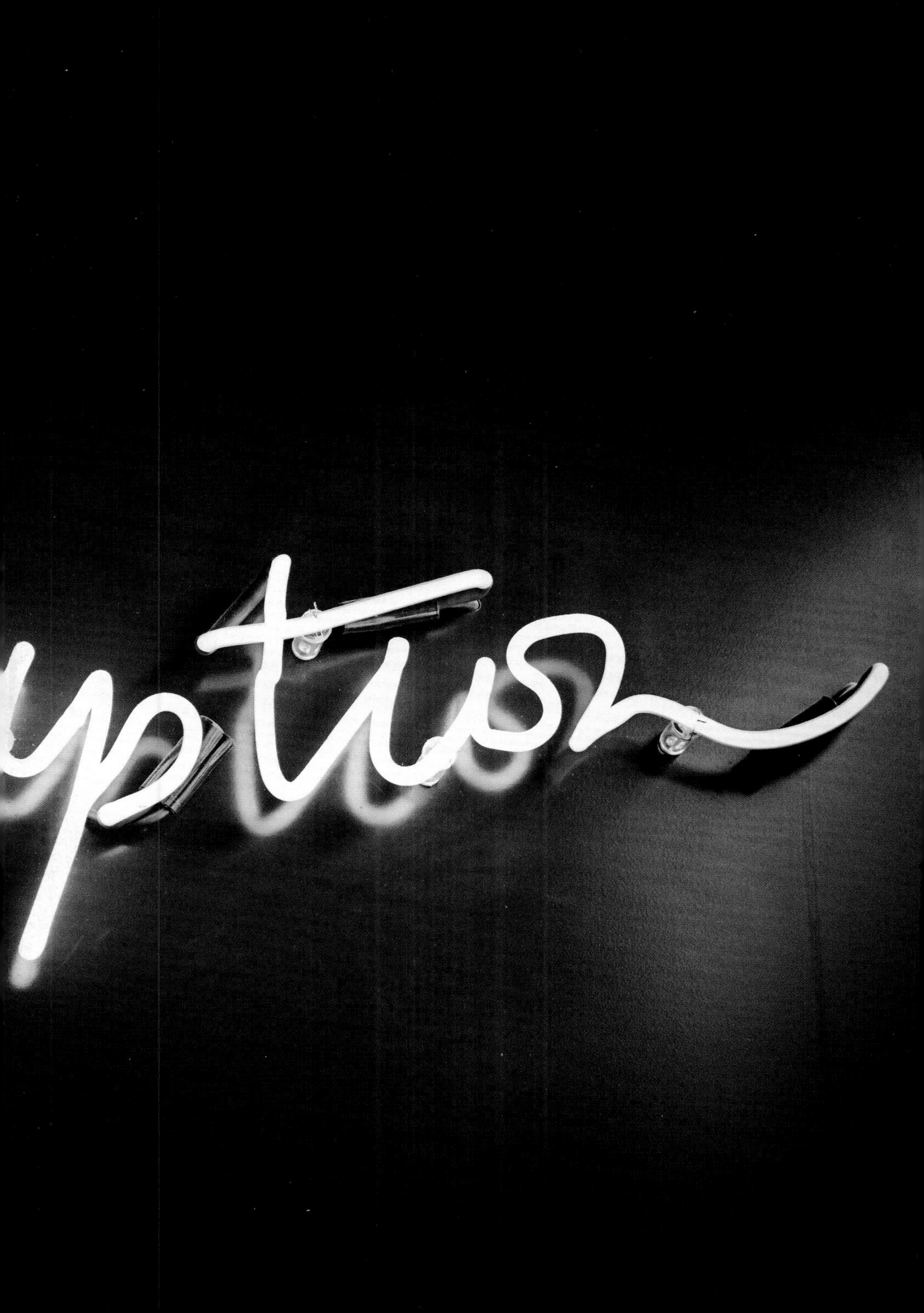

To Kay Madden and Ali Salway, who are the wind beneath our (angel) wings.

An Hachette UK Company
www.hachette.co.uk
First published in Great Britain in 2018 by
Kyle Books, an imprint of Kyle Cathie Ltd
Carmelite House
50 Victoria Embankment
London EC4Y 0DZ
www.kylebooks.co.uk

ISBN: 978 0 85783 569 7

Distributed in the US by Hachette Book Group,
1290 Avenue of the Americas,
4th and 5th Floors, New York, NY 10104

Distributed in Canada by Canadian Manda Group,
664 Annette St., Toronto, Ontario, Canada M6S 2C8

Editor: Tara O'Sullivan
Editorial Assistant: Sarah Kyle
Design: Evi O Studio
Photography: Catherine Gratwicke
Food styling: Andrea Waters
Props styling: Agathe Gits
Production: Nic Jones and Gemma John

Printed and bound in China

10 9 8 7 6 5 4 3 2 1

INTRODUCTION

Cocktail bars conjure up powerfully seductive images in our minds. For us women it goes something like this... We strut in wearing a sophisticated outfit in a waft of expensive perfume, slide onto a bar stool, and look a million dollars in the glamorous lighting. The handsome barman begins to mix our martini. A charming stranger starts to engage us in a sizzling conversation...

Before we get carried away, we should point out that we've drunk in some of the best bars in the world and, unfortunately, we have very rarely managed to pull off this particular scenario! And yet the allure remains.

It's also a huge amount of fun to create your own cocktail party, whether that be for a birthday, Christmas, New Year's Eve, engagement, wedding, baby shower – or simply because it's Saturday night!

We love the energy these amazing spaces and parties can create, but why can't you have that without the sugar and the alcohol? Many of us love a good knees-up, but why should socializing *always* be at the expense of your health?

This was the question behind the thinking process that formed Redemption.

CATHERINE For me, this all started when I was working at Virgin, looking after the brand and launching lots of businesses around the world. I saw some really interesting trends such as the modern hippy chic developing out of Byron Bay, Australia, and the constant adoption of LA health and beauty ideas (which people first dismissed as fads) into worldwide movements. Young Italians taught me a thing or two about alcohol – for them, it's considered embarrassing to be seen as drunk, and they would flirt in the gyms in Rome and Milan like you would in nightclubs in the UK. It was sexy to be healthy.

London had a real party culture at the time I joined Virgin – it was the '90s, we were young, we had fantastic creative jobs, we were working hard and playing hard too. What started out as raucous fun started to become a rather toxic lifestyle: roll on 17 years, and drinking too much and eating too much had kind of crept up on me. The catalyst came from me after a difficult break up that left me questioning my relationship with alcohol. I knew I wanted to make some changes, so I left my Virgin job and went on a yoga retreat to Goa in India (as you do) and there I stayed in a place where there was no alcohol at all. I noticed how liberated I felt when freed from the constant temptation. All these things were swirling around in my mind and the more research I did, the more it pointed to the fact that there was a gap in the market. If you wanted to make a lifestyle change, or had simply been on a healthy holiday like I had and wanted to keep up the good work, there weren't any restaurants or bars back in London where you could do that.

The trends and the research I was picking up on at the time have since grown even stronger. The older generation are realizing they need to drink less alcohol and are constantly being told to cut back. The younger generation coming through are less enamoured with alcohol. There's quite a few reasons for that: some have seen their parents drunk (not cool); they care about their image a lot; and with the dominance of social media the pub is no longer the cultural hub and rite of passage it once was. But we also like to think it goes deeper than that – there is a rising consciousness about taking more responsibility for how your actions affect yourself, others, animals and the planet.

I began chatting to nutritional therapists (I still hadn't met Andrea at this point), and they were all of the view that next to alcohol, refined sugar was probably one of the next most damaging things. Most people agreed that a diet which was plant-based (certainly plant-centric) was the healthiest route to go down. So I did a couple of pop-ups to test the market with a plant-based, alcohol-free, sugar-free offering – one on the roof in Netil House Hackney and the other underneath Trellick Tower in Portobello. The nutritional therapist I was working with knew Andrea, we were introduced, and we hit it off straight away. She was the expert that Redemption needed. She was doing a full-time social enterprise project but she had this amazing 'Can Do' attitude and she helped on the third and final pop-up, designing the food and drinks menu and helping to recruit the team. This meant I was able to focus on getting a permanent location and raising capital. Over the course of a year, it became pretty obvious that we were ideally suited to become business partners and create the Redemption vision together.

ANDREA I grew up in a '70s pool party house filled with Boney M., sideburns, muumuus and glacé cherries. However much my parents loved to entertain, there was a wholesome balance to my childhood view of the world. I was lucky to grow up in a place that lived up to its name, The Bay of Plenty, New Zealand, with its sub-tropical weather, fertile land and plentiful sea. My wonderful father worked closely with many Maori from the Te Whakatōhea tribe and our family was invited as VIP guests to share their Hangis on special occasions. We learnt through the Maori culture to understand the value of environmental protectionism. Unlike most religions the Maori worship Earth Mother and Sky Father and acknowledge the value of our relationship with nature.

I have strong memories of my mother and grandfather teaching me to live with the seasons, harvesting gluts of fruit or vegetables and making preserves and chutneys, bottling, labelling and enjoying the fruits of our labour. I learnt to cook at my mother's side – she was an exceptional and experimental cook.

My grandmother was an intellectual bohemian. She loved music, history and politics, she was glamorous and fun but, on reflection, she was dependent on alcohol as self-medication for the relief of both physical and emotional pain. I thought the world of her, but I admit she wasn't always easy to manage after a few drinks.

Working in the hospitality industry for more years than I'm prepared to admit, I have witnessed the damage that the over-consumption of – and addiction to – alcohol has caused to some of my colleagues, and consequently their relationships with family and friends. During the '90s, I felt that there was a big drinking culture within the industry. After we'd finished our shifts, we'd stay on and drink in the bars, and sometimes drink 'team cocktails' until the sun came up before trying to make it to work the next day to do it all again. One bar manager used to secretly pour her cocktails in the pot plants at team events just to appear to fit in! Thankfully times have changed and the expectation to drink at work events has diminished, but it has not disappeared entirely. If there was an elixir that could allow you to lose weight, help you sleep better, improve your skin and memory, and generally make you more attractive, it would become an overnight sensation. But there isn't a magic elixir – all you have to do to achieve all these benefits is stop drinking alcohol! Of course there are numerous other benefits to giving up or reducing your alcohol intake, ranging from better decision-making when socializing, to protecting yourself from long-term memory impairment, brain damage, liver disease and, in women, breast cancer. Ironically the initial 'magical' uplifting effects of drinking alcohol makes it very easy to forget that alcohol is actually a depressant and has the ability to exacerbate underlying mental health disorders. But we're not here to preach to you – we just want to show you another way.

I am honoured to have met Catherine and been given the opportunity to create a space I would have proudly taken my grandmother to. She would have loved the buzz, the music and the philosophy of Redemption. We love the idea that it is not only possible to socialise without it being at the expense of your health, but it's glamorous and fun. In our bars we wanted to give the cocktail experience without the downside. Our aim is for the brain's reward centre to be enticed and satiated, without experiencing the lows. We are proud of creating a thriving restaurant/bar business that isn't fuelled on alcohol and provides a safe place for our customers and also for our staff to work.

ABOUT OUR BOOK

We've put together some of our best drinks ideas into this book so that you can create something truly magical with no toxins and temptations. On top of that, we've given you a taster of our favourite canapés so you can create some scrumptious and sophisticated nibbles to serve alongside the drinks.

Customers of Redemption will spot some favourites from our restaurant bars in here, such as the Apple Mockjito, Fro-co-rita and Flu Fighters Martini, which have been on the menu from the early days. We've also designed some new drinks which we hope to put on the menu in the near future.

EQUIPMENT

In the restaurant bars we rely heavily on having the right equipment for the job, but we also like them to look beautiful to add to the theatre of cocktail making. We love copper cocktail shakers and muddlers to display on the bar. The serious bit of kit to consider is which blender to use. We have a Vitamix (which cost the same as Catherine's first car – a bit out of the price range of the amateur) but all the bar staff love the Nutribullet because it's easy to clean and it's the perfect size for making just a couple of drinks. We buy our beautiful glassware from a catering supplier because it has to be robust for restaurant use, but you'll see from this book that we love nothing more than to rummage around in charity shops for gorgeous, vintage finds and put it all together an exciting and eclectic display.

INGREDIENT GLOSSARY

Here are just a few of the key ingredients you'll find throughout the book.

APPLE CIDER VINEGAR has undergone fermentation to form health-promoting probiotics and enzymes. It is important to make sure the vinegar you buy is organic and raw (sometimes labelled as containing 'the mother'). You need to drink only 2 tablespoons each day to take advantage of the myriad health benefits.

AQUAFABA is the viscous liquid from tinned chickpeas, otherwise known as 'vegan egg whites', and it can be used for many of the same things, from meringues to frothing up cocktails. Next time you drain a tin of chickpeas, instead of throwing the liquid away, pour it into ice cube trays and freeze.

BIRCH WATER is tapped from birch trees in the same way as maple syrup. It's a refreshing drink with a distinctive but delicate taste.

CACAO POWDER might look and taste like cocoa powder, but there's a world of difference nutritionally. Cacao is made from cold-pressed cacao beans, a process which preserves all the nutrients, calcium, magnesium flavanoids, zinc, iron, potassium and manganese. Cocoa powder, on the other hand, is roasted at very high temperatures which destroys the nutrients.

COCONUT SUGAR has a lower glycaemic index than refined table sugar and contains inulin (which may slow glucose absorption), iron, zinc, calcium and potassium. Plus, it tastes like caramel!

COCONUT WATER is found in the centre of young, green coconuts. It supports liver and heart health and reduces blood pressure. It's great after working out as it hydrates and replaces the electrolytes lost during exercise.

GINGER has long been a favourite for its anti-inflammatory properties and ability to calm the gut and relieve nausea. It helps to strengthen the immune system, ramp up metabolism and support memory function.

HIBISCUS FLOWERS are a beautiful deep red colour, and contain vitamin C and minerals. They are used traditionally as a gentle medicine.

HIMALAYAN SALT is one of the purest salts and contains over 84 minerals and trace elements.

MAPLE SYRUP contains zinc and manganese, with the addition of potassium and calcium.

MEDJOOL DATES are our preferred sweetener. They're full of potassium, copper and manganese, and the fructose is contained within the whole fruit so is better absorbed by the body alongside all of the goodness.

POMEGRANATES provide us with a wealth of antioxidants and phytochemicals that help to challenge free radicals and protect our cells. They also taste and look beautiful – the jewel-like seeds make a perfect garnish, and pomegranate molasses is pleasing balance of sweet and sharp.

XYLITOL might sound like a freaky chemical, but it's actually just the dried sap from birch trees. If you haven't used it yet, we recommend you start. It's great for replacing traditional sugar in our recipes because it contains 40 per cent less calories (not that we're counting, but 40!). It's also good for your oral health – far from the damaging effects of sugar on your teeth, xylitol has actually been shown to improve rather than cause decay.

I

SHRUBS, FERMENTS & CORDIALS

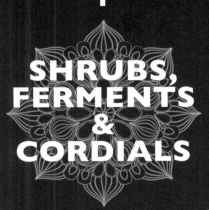

The recipes in this chapter will form a basis for many of the drinks later on, and enable you to build up a shelf of homemade cocktail ingredients.

Shrubs, or drinking vinegars, are essentially a mixture of fruits, sugar (in our case xylitol – see page 12) and vinegar. Pre-refrigeration, vinegar was a perfect preserver for seasonal fruit and vegetables, and making a syrup with sugar meant the glut of ripe fruits at harvest time could be enjoyed long into the winter months – they will keep for up to a year, although the flavours change and develop with time. With the advent of refrigeration, the practice of shrubbing died out, and has only recently made a comeback in experimental cocktail bars.

The cordials are worth making for everyday drinking as well as for use in cocktails – just top with chilled sparkling water as an alternative to chemical-laden canned soft drinks.

We hope once you have mastered the basic principles of making these recipes you will start experimenting and create some interesting ones of your own. Do aim to use fresh, in-season fruits and vegetables as the flavour (and price) will be best.

HIBISCUS CORDIAL

We love escaping to Ibiza whenever we can. With the pressures of running a busy bar, we can't get away that often these days, but this cordial transports us immediately to glorious summers on the white isle, bringing to mind the gorgeous sight of the hibiscus bushes flowering with their startling splashes of bright red, pink, yellow and deep purple. Unlike the party revellers, who sleep in the day and blossom at night, the hibiscus comes out to play in the sunlight but closes its petals to the world when the sun goes down.

Dried hibiscus flowers can be enjoyed wherever you are in the world, made into a wonderful deep magenta-coloured infusion that can be drunk hot or cold, with or without sweetener.

COOK   35 minutes
MAKES   approx 750ml
        (1¹/₃ pints)

50g (1¾oz) dried hibiscus flowers (you can use 10 hibiscus tea bags instead, but you won't end up with the lovely flowers for garnishing)
300g (10½oz) xylitol (see page 12)
1.5 litres (2¾ pints) filtered water
juice of 2 limes
2 vanilla pods (optional)

Put the dried hibiscus flowers, xylitol and water into a saucepan and bring to the boil. Reduce the heat and leave to simmer for 30 minutes, then remove from the heat and cool. Once cooled, strain the juice into a jug and set the hibiscus flowers aside for later.

Add the lime juice to the jug and stir.

Pop a couple of the reserved hibiscus flowers and the vanilla pods (if using) into a sterilised 75cl bottle (see below), then top up with the cordial. Seal and store in the fridge for up to four weeks. The cordial can be enjoyed simply over ice and topped with sparkling water, or added to cocktails.

Note

STERILISING BOTTLES AND JARS Bottles and jars for food and drink need to be sterilised even if they are brand new. Either place rinsed bottles and jars in your dishwasher on the hottest cycle, or wash and rinse in hot water, then dry out in a preheated oven at 140°C/275°F for 15–20 minutes. Remember to pour hot liquids into hot bottles and cool liquids into cool bottles.

HISBISCUS FLOWERS IN SYRUP

MAKES 1 SMALL JAR

Hibiscus flowers in syrup are such a gorgeous drink garnish although rather expensive to buy and not widely available. Good news! After making the Hibiscus cordial you have lots of lovely Hibiscus flowers begging to be turned into frivolous cocktail adornments at very little cost.

Put the reserved hibiscus flowers into a sterilised jar (see left) and set aside. Put 300g (10½oz) xylitol and 250ml (9fl oz) filtered water into a small saucepan and bring to a boil, stirring from time to time to help the xylitol dissolve. Once it has dissolved, let the syrup simmer for 5 minutes, then remove from the heat and allow to cool slightly before pouring over the flowers. Leave to cool, then keep in the fridge and use to add glamour to the drinks of your choice. They will keep for about a month.

PEAR AND LEMON
THYME SHRUB

Shrub, or drinking vinegar, became popular during America's colonial era — essentially because it was a great way of preserving soft fruits by marinating them in vinegar and sugar. The fruits would be eaten separately, and the remaining syrup enjoyed topped with water or soda water as a refreshing long drink. Shrubs eventually fell out of fashion with the arrival of home refrigeration for berries and the rise of more convenient shop-bought refreshments. Recently the world's top bars 'in the know' have boasted homemade shrubs as part of their bar collection. The acidity of this tart little shrub makes it well suited as an apéritif or as an alternative to bitters in cocktails.

PREP   20 minutes
MACERATING + WAITING
TIME   7 days
MAKES   500ml (18fl oz)

3 unripe pears, washed,
   cored and diced
6 lemon thyme sprigs,
   rinsed
1 tablespoon juniper
   berries, slightly
   crushed
strips of zest from
   1 unwaxed lemon
50g (1¾oz) fresh ginger,
   peeled and grated
200g (7oz) xylitol (see
   page 12)
250ml (9fl oz) raw apple
   cider vinegar

Put the pears, thyme, juniper berries, lemon strips, ginger and xylitol into a large sterilised jar (see page 16) and stir well to combine.

Close the jar and refrigerate for 24 hours to macerate so the flavours blend together. Add the apple cider vinegar and seal with the lid (see Note below), then shake gently to combine. Store in the fridge for 6 days before use.

After 6 days, strain the liquid through a fine-mesh sieve, pour into a sterilised bottle or jar and seal with the lid. This will keep in the fridge for up to a year. The shrub can be enjoyed simply over ice and topped with sparkling water, or added to cocktails.

You can save the slightly pickled pears in a separate container in the fridge and use in a salad, with crunchy, curly endive salad leaves, roasted beetroot, orange segments, black olives and toasted pecans.

Note

All recipes containing vinegar require a container with a non-reactive lid, such as glass. If the jar you are using has a metal lid, place a piece of new baking parchment or waxed paper between the lid and the liquid. This helps prevent the vinegar from corroding the lid.

LEMONGRASS AND CHILLI SHRUB

Lemongrass grows like wildfire in the hot climates of Thailand and Vietnam and in Andrea's Aunty Jaja's garden in Queensland, Australia. You might be surprised to learn that this fragrant culinary grass also grows happily in temperate climates such as the UK, as long as you bring it inside over winter. The easiest way to grow lemongrass is from fresh stalks, so why not use the lemongrass tops in this recipe and see if you can get the base of the stalk to root.

PREP	10 minutes
COOK	5 minutes
FERMENT	7 days
MAKES	750ml (1¹/₃ pints)

5–6 lemongrass stalks (extra if using the base to root plants)
1 unwaxed lemon, cut into wedges
1 large chilli, seeds intact, trimmed
250ml (9fl oz) maple syrup
500ml (18fl oz) raw apple cider vinegar

Roughly chop the lemongrass stalks, lemon wedges and chilli and put in a large sterilised jar (see page 16). Muddle the mixture with a wooden spoon, then add the maple syrup.

Pour the apple cider vinegar into a saucepan and warm gently over a low heat, bringing it to 45°C/113°F on a food thermometer.

Pour the warm apple cider vinegar into the jar. Cover with a non-reactive lid (see Note, page 18) and shake to mix.

Leave to steep in the fridge for a week, shaking the jar every 2–3 days.

Strain the shrub through a fine sieve and transfer to a sterilised bottle. This will keep in the fridge for up to a year. This refreshing shrub can be enjoyed simply over ice and topped with sparkling water, or added to cocktails for extra zing.

MAPLE AND GINGER SWITCHEL

A thirst-quenching beverage that functions much like a sports drink*, replacing the potassium (an electrolyte) and sugars lost through sweat, except that this is made with raw apple cider vinegar, pure maple syrup and fresh ginger, topped up with water. All the ingredients are great sources of potassium.

Vinegar may seem an odd ingredient for a beverage, but many traditional drink recipes call for vinegar, either to preserve or replace fruit. In a switchel, the apple cider vinegar provides a lovely tanginess similar to citrus fruit and, when mixed with maple syrup and spicy ginger, it's delicious – rather like a ginger ale.

PREP   15 minutes
CHILL   2 hours
MAKES   I litre

500ml (18fl oz) raw apple
  cider vinegar
100g (3½ oz) fresh ginger,
  peeled and roughly sliced
500ml (18fl oz) maple
  syrup

TO SERVE
sparkling mineral water

Put the apple cider vinegar and ginger in a blender and blitz until it forms a purée.

Pass the ginger mixture through a fine sieve or a nut bag over a bowl, aiming to extract as much of the liquid as possible. Add the maple syrup and mix (add more or less to your taste).

Pour into a sterilised bottle (see page 16). Chill for at least 2 hours before tasting. This will keep well in the fridge for up to 2 months.

To serve, just add chilled sparkling mineral water for a simple refreshing spritzer. You can also use this as a cocktail ingredient – see Cinderella on page 56 or Basil and Blackberry Bramble on page 62.

Note

* Triathlons are undertaken at the reader's own risk!

GRENADINE

ANDREA My memories of grenadine are tied up with my parent's legendary parties of the '70s, my father sporting a khaki safari suit and sideburns, my mother wafting around in a bright muumuu, Boney M.'s 'Daddy Cool' on full blast. My brother and I thought we were the bee's knees, knocking back our Shirley Temples, which were made from soda stream ginger ale, a good slug of the neon red grenadine from Dad's bar and a garish garnish of orange twist and maraschino cherry. Judging by the adults' dance moves, they were very clearly indulging in drinks of a much stronger nature than ours.

That grenadine was largely made up of artificial flavouring, lots of sugar and bright red food dye, not to mention a whole list of unpronounceable chemicals. On reflection, it probably would have been healthier had my parents allowed us to drink sherry with our grandmother on the sofa.

At Redemption we make proper grenadine from pomegranates, which is ruby red and simultaneously sweet and tart. It might seem like a bit of a faff, but it's well worth making this with fresh pomegranate seeds for their nutritional value.

PREP	30 minutes
COOK	15 minutes
MAKES	750ml (1¹/₃ pints)

500g (18oz) pomegranate seeds
500ml (18fl oz) filtered water
300g (10½oz) xylitol (see page 12)
60ml (4 tablespoons) pomegranate molasses (available at most supermarkets and health food stores)
1 teaspoon orange blossom water

Put the pomegranate seeds and the measured water in a non-reactive saucepan over a medium heat, and bring to a simmer.

Using a potato masher, crush the seeds gently to release the juice. This is preferable to blending them, as their white cores release a rather bitter taste if overcrushed.

Add the xylitol and simmer for 10 minutes, stirring occasionally to dissolve.

Strain the liquid through a sieve into a bowl, using a ladle to push and pass the pomegranate juice through the mesh, discarding the hard white core of the seeds. Add the pomegranate molasses and the orange blossom water, and mix well.

Let (Daddy) cool, then transfer to a sterilised bottle (see page 16). This will keep in the fridge for up to 1 month.

COCONUT WATER KEFIR

CATHERINE 'Who fancies a lacto-fermented beverage?' wasn't something I would hear myself saying until I met Andrea.

ANDREA Water kefir is an incredibly easy vegan alternative to milk kefir and you can be enjoying your first lacto-fermented* beverage within a week. We continuously have fermentations bubbling away in the restaurants, as I do at home. Catherine often cautiously picks up one of the mysterious potions that percolate in my kitchen and tries to work out what on earth it is for. To me they are a thing of beauty – my pets, I guess – I look after them well so they will look after me. Kefir has a plethora of health benefits. The probiotic bacteria created in the fermenting process aids detoxification and supports gut health, which in turn boosts mental wellbeing.

I suggest you buy dehydrated kefir grains online or at your local health food store. These will need to be activated for three days at room temperature before you can start making kefir.

MAKES   approx. I litre

500ml (18fl oz) boiled and
  cooled filtered water
40g (1½oz) sugar (we use
  coconut sugar)
I x 60g (2oz) sachet
  dehydrated water kefir
  grains

EQUIPMENT
I-litre sterilised glass jar
  with lid

STAGE ONE – ACTIVATION

Mix together the measured water and sugar until the sugar has dissolved.

Pour the sugar water into the sterilised glass jar (see page 16) and add the dehydrated kefir grains.

Place a clean piece of cloth or kitchen paper over the jar and secure with an elastic band.

Leave at room temperature for 3 days, then drain, discarding the sugar water and reserving the activated kefir grains.

Note

* 'lacto-fermented' is not to be confused with lactose, which is the sugar in milk.

CONTINUED OVERLEAF

STAGE TWO — BREWING

1 litre (1¾ pints) boiled
and cooled filtered water
80g (3oz) sugar (we use
coconut sugar)
your activated kefir grains
(see page 25)

EQUIPMENT
2-litre sterilised glass jar
with lid
sterilised bottles with
lids for storing the
finished kefir

Mix the measured water and coconut sugar until the sugar has dissolved.

Pour the sugar water into the sterilised glass jar (see page 16) and add the activated kefir grains.

Place a clean piece of cloth or kitchen paper over the jar and secure with an elastic band. Leave at room temperature for 48 hours.

Now separate the kefir water from the grains using a plastic sieve to filter. Pour the kefir water into sterilised bottles and refrigerate for 12 hours before drinking.

Rinse the grains in boiled and cooled filtered water. Re-sterilise the jar and return the grains to the jar. Repeat the above process every 48 hours to give you a continuous supply of kefir water.

Tips

Chlorinated tap water can be harmful to the kefir grains. It's best to use filtered water that has been boiled and then cooled. Boiling and cooling in an open saucepan is best, as it allows the chlorine to evaporate more effectively.

Look after your kefir grains – avoid metal utensils, use bamboo or plastic sieves and sterilise your jars between batches.

Keep your kefir away from direct sunlight.

Remember kefir grains are (once activated) alive, and are hungry little things, so you must keep them well fed!

KOMBUCHA

You could write a whole book on kombucha. It's been booming in popularity recently and is even catching on in high street food chains, so you can expect to see a lot of it about. Here is Andrea's quick guide:

Kombucha is a fermented tea that is known to have originated about 2,000 years ago. It contains probiotics, beneficial enzymes and B vitamins. Its benefits include better liver detoxification, improved digestion and nutrient assimiliation, improved joint health, increased energy, reduced candida and enhanced mood. So it's well worth giving it a try!

I had always assumed that the art of brewing kombucha was really complicated and that so much could go wrong – until my Australian outback cousin revealed he'd been brewing it for years, and I realised if he could get cultured, then so could I.

I invested in a large earthenware kombucha crock with a spigot, and of course it sat there empty, mocking me for months, and finally I hid it away in the cupboard and continued to buy ready-made kombucha.

Then we started running fermentation workshops at Redemption and the whole kombucha issue fizzed up again. I was embarrassed that I needed to be reminded how easy and cheap it is to make this immortal health elixir.

So, out comes the crock with spigot. There are plenty of different styles of crock out there – glazed earthenware, glass and porcelain. I prefer glazed earthenware as I don't want to have floating SCOBY (Symbiotic Culture of Bacteria and Yeast) on full view in my kitchen – they do look very odd, almost alien. However, you can opt for a glass crock if you have a sense of the macabre. A SCOBY is a symbiosis of algae and fungus called a lichen. The SCOBY feeds on sweetened tea to produce a fermented tonic that contains a host of beneficial bacteria, yeasts and acids. You can buy a SCOBY online or in many health food shops, but the best way to get a SCOBY is from someone who is already brewing kombucha, as the lichen is prolific and produces offspring every week. So keep your SCOBY healthy and you too will be proudly gifting little baby lichens to all your friends... no gift wrapping required!

The continuous brew method is by far the most straightforward way – it speeds up the brewing time, has a better overall taste and reduces the risks of mould or spoilage.

SHRUBS, FERMENTS & CORDIALS

CONTINUED OVERLEAF

KOMBUCHA CONTINUED

PREP   20 minutes
FERMENT 7–21 days
MAKES   approx. 2.5 litres

2.25 litres (4 pints) filtered
  water
4 organic green tea bags
160g (5½oz) organic
  unrefined granulated
  sugar
200ml (6½fl oz) raw
  unpasteurised kombucha
1 healthy SCOBY
  (see page 27)

Tip

Take care when opening
the bottles – as with all
fizzy drinks, there is a risk
of an eruption.

Boil the measured water, steep the tea bags
and add the sugar. Remove the tea bags after
10 minutes. So far so easy! Cool the tea.

Pour the cooled tea into the crock, filling to
the three-quarters level. Add 200ml (6½fl oz)
kombucha. With very clean hands, add the
SCOBY.

Cover the jar with a fermentation cover or
use a coffee filter secured with an elastic band.
Put the jar in the corner of the kitchen where
it is at least a metre away from any other
fermenting products. Leave to ferment for
7–21 days – though the length of time may vary
depending on the ambient temperature and
batch size. You can taste test the kombucha
to see if it is done. It should be a balanced taste
of tart but still slightly sweet.

At this point, the kombucha is ready for
a second ferment.

As we are using the continuous brew method,
we dispense the liquid through the spigot
(this allows you to remove the kombucha
without the need to disturb the SCOBY) into
large sterilised flip top brewing bottles, leaving
about 2–5cm of the bottle unfilled.

If you like you can add a few pieces of naturally dried fruit (without sulphur dioxide preservative), citrus peel or fresh fruit chunks. This will gently flavour your 'buch' and also give a little extra sugar to aid the second fermentation. Do make sure there is still 2cm (¾ in) left unfilled.

Seal your bottles and leave at room temperature for 7–14 days. The warmer the room and the more fruit (sugar) the shorter the 'fizz-time'. In cooler weather, it could take the full 2 weeks.

I like to fill one plastic bottle as a control bottle to watch. As the carbonation happens, the plastic gets tight and it is obvious when the 'buch' is ready without having to open your glass bottles to check every few days and lose that precious carbonation that has built up.

This also helps prevent the chance of your bottle exploding (!) as you can transfer it into the fridge before it over ferments. Once in the fridge, the fermentation slows down to hibernation speed.

Drink once chilled. It will keep for at least 3 months, but as it ages the flavour will develop and will become drier as the sugars are slowly digested. After a few trials you'll decide how long you need to leave it till the flavour is to your taste.

Now go back to the beginning of the recipe and make the sweetened tea, top up the crock to start first fermentation again. Bottle, chill, drink and repeat... happily ever after.

RHUBARB CORDIAL

For some, rhubarb is as quintessentially English as cricket on the lawn and cucumber sandwiches at the rectory, although it's actually thought to have originated in China and been taken along the Silk Road to Europe in the fourteenth century. Although rhubarb is available almost all year round, for our recipes we favour the cultivated (or 'forced' rhubarb) with its bright pink, tender stalks. Most of this rhubarb sold in the UK comes from within the so-called 'Rhubarb Triangle' between the towns of Wakefield, Morley and Rothwell in West Yorkshire. Rhubarb crowns grown outdoors are transferred to heated sheds and kept in darkness, which forces the growth and produces more delicate and sweeter stalks with their distinctive pale crimson colour.

PREP	20 minutes + overnight straining
COOK	30 minutes
MAKES	2 litres (3½ pints)

2kg (4lb 8oz) young pink rhubarb stems, washed well and sliced

250ml (9fl oz) freshly squeezed orange juice

2cm (¾ in) piece fresh ginger, peeled and sliced

1.5 litres (2¾ pints) filtered water

700g (1lb 9oz) xylitol (see page 12)

Put the rhubarb, orange juice, ginger and water in a large non-reactive saucepan.

Bring to the boil, then reduce the heat to a simmer for 15 minutes.

Allow to cool, then transfer to a jelly bag over a large bowl and leave overnight to strain (save the rhubarb pulp for a delicious coconut yogurt rhubarb fool).

Pour the rhubarb juice back into the pan and add the xylitol. Bring to a simmer, stirring until the xylitol dissolves.

Bottle and store in the fridge until required and for up to 3 weeks.

CHERRY CORDIAL

As Doris Day sang, 'Life is just a bowl of cherries. Don't take it serious; it's too mysterious.' If life was indeed a bowl of cherries it would be bursting with intense, albeit somewhat short-lived, flavour and brightness. Perhaps one of the reasons we love fresh cherries is because they remain mysterious and unavailable for much of the year – even the most well-stocked markets can only get their hands on them in June or December, from either hemisphere. So, do make sure you enjoy their explosive juiciness when they are in season. In this recipe, we add cracked cherry stones to the pot of fruit, which imparts a lovely almond flavour to the cordial. Try with and without to see which you prefer.

PREP	40 minutes
COOK	30 minutes
MAKES	1 litre (1¾ pints)

500g (1lb 2oz) ripe dark
  Morello cherries
100g (3½ oz) xylitol
juice of 1 lemon
500ml (18fl oz) filtered
  water

Wash the cherries and remove the stones. Place the stones in a square of muslin and tie it up around them, then bash with a rolling pin to slightly crack open the stones.

Put the pitted cherries, muslin bag of stones, xylitol, lemon juice and water in a preserving pan or large saucepan over a medium heat. Stir gently and bring to the boil, reduce the heat and simmer for 10 minutes then remove the bag of stones. Continue simmering the cherries for a further 15 minutes.

Blitz in a blender then pass through a fine-mesh sieve, extracting as much liquid as you can. Pour into a sterilised (see page 16) bottle and refrigerate.

The cordial will keep for at least 2 weeks in the fridge. Use in cocktails or serve simply with lots of crushed ice and sparkling mineral water.

QUICK GINGERED TEPACHE

SHRUBS, FERMENTS & CORDIALS

Tepache is a Mexican drink made from slightly fermented pineapple and it's loaded with enzymes and vitamins. Served over ice it is a great way to cool off on long summer days. In Mexico, tepache is traditionally made using just the pineapple skin and core. Because these parts of the fruit are usually discarded we like to stick to tradition and minimise waste. You can, however, add some of the chopped fruit if you wish.

CATHERINE I wish I had known about this drink when I was a plus-one to a house music DJ on a tour around the gorgeous Tulum area in Mexico, just before we launched Redemption. I was drinking tequila by night and weapons-grade coffee by day, which probably explains why we ended up having a sun-drenched kaleidoscopic argument. Tepache would have been a much better idea.

PREP   15 minutes
FERMENT 48 hours
MAKES   1 litre (1¾ pints)

1 large ripe pineapple
125ml (4fl oz) máple syrup
1 cinnamon stick
50g (1¾oz) fresh ginger,
   peeled and sliced
1 litre (1¾ pints) filtered
   water

Wash the pineapple well, then peel off the skin and set aside. Cut the peeled fruit into quarters. Remove the core and set aside with the skin.

Cut the rest of the pineapple into slices or chunks and store either in the fridge to eat later or pop into the freezer to use in smoothies.

Place the sliced core and skin in a large glass jar with the rest of the ingredients. Stir to combine, cover with a thin tea towel or cloth and secure with an elastic band or string. Allow the mixture to sit for 24 hours at room temperature.

Remove the white foam that will form, re-cover, and leave to ferment for a further 24 hours: any longer and it will become slightly alcoholic, and if you allow it to ferment beyond that period it will probably end up as pineapple vinegar.

Strain and chill in the fridge before serving. It will keep for 2 weeks, stored in the fridge.

2

CLASSICS

It was quite a task to categorise cocktails in relevant sections as many fall into several… In the end, we decided that those cocktails that made it into our Classics chapter had to have a little bit of history that really engages us. With that in mind, these are our 'classics'.

BLOODY MARY — invented in the 1920s by Fernand Petiot, a barman working in Paris. He took the recipe to New York in the early '30s. The New Yorkers thought the drink a little bland and asked him to spice it up — and a modern classic was born.

MIMOSA — another classic from Paris in the 1920s, this time from the barman Frank Meier at Hotel Ritz. It's believed to be named after the gorgeous yellow flowers of the same name.

DAIQUIRI — Hemingway insisted on his cocktails being ice cold and loved a frozen daiquiri.
In *Islands in the Stream* he describes, 'this frozen daiquiri, so well beaten as it is, looks like the sea where the wave falls away from the bow of a ship when doing thirty knots'.

PUNCH — a Sanskrit word meaning five, the drink was originally made from five simple ingredients, bought to England by sailors working for the British East India Company in the seventeenth century. Our alcohol-free version is classic in its five ingredients and gives you all the punch without being knocked out!

PIÑA COLADA — 'Yes I like piña coladas, and getting caught in the rain.' As a nation, the British have put piña colada at the top of the cocktail charts since the '80s. Hard not to get caught in the rain if you live here.

HERITAGE TOMATO BLOODY MARY

You don't actually have to have a hangover to enjoy a good Bloody Mary. This is a really special one – rich, hot, and packed full of nutrients. When you make your own tomato juice, you know it's free of preservatives and additives. Juice can be made from any type of tomatoes, but we love Isle of Wight heritage tomatoes. Mass-produced hybrid G tomatoes look perfect but tend to have less flavour when compared to the heritage or old-fashioned varieties. Ripeness is key, so look for fruit that is plump, bright in colour, and has flesh that gives to the touch.

PREP   15 minutes
CHILL   12–24 hours
SERVES   10

3kg (6lb 8oz) ripe heritage
   tomatoes (we use a
   mix of cherry, tiger
   and piccolo), coarsely
   chopped
4 celery sticks, coarsely
   chopped
2 red peppers, roughly
   chopped
1 red chilli, deseeded
2 tablespoons finely grated
   fresh horseradish
1 tablespoon fine
   Himalayan salt

TO SERVE
1 tablespoon Tabasco sauce
1 tablespoon vegan
   Worcestershire sauce
juice of 1 large lemon
   (about 4 tablespoons)

TO GARNISH
long and leafy celery sticks
micro tomatoes (optional)
freshly ground black pepper

The day before you want to serve, blitz the tomatoes with the other ingredients, working in small batches, in a food processor or blender until smooth.

Transfer to a jug and chill overnight.

Strain the juice through a very fine sieve (save any pulp in your freezer to add to soups or pasta sauces).

To serve, add the Tabasco, Worcestershire sauce and lemon juice to the tomato juice mixture and stir.

Half-fill highball glasses with ice, add a stick of leafy celery, then pour in the tomato juice mix. Grind black pepper on the top, garnish with micro tomatoes (if using) and serve.

PIOUS PIÑA COLADA

A Piña Colada always seems like such a good idea when you first get on your Caribbean sunlounger at about 11am. But then it sadly arrives in a plastic poolside cup with a glacé cherry, and you're left with a sticky mouth and a headache. We actually prefer our pious version – it has a beautiful creamy balance of tropical fruitiness and a zesty tang. This will definitely be on the menu when we open Redemption in St Lucia.

PREP 5 minutes
SERVES 1

160g (5½oz) fresh pineapple chunks
coconut blossom nectar, for dipping (available in health food stores and online)
1 tablespoon freshly squeezed lemon juice
50ml (2fl oz) Coconut Water Kefir (see page 25)
1 rounded tablespoon coconut yogurt
50ml (2fl oz) organic coconut milk
a few large ice cubes

TO GARNISH
a thin wedge of fresh pineapple
pineapple leaf (optional)

Rub a chunk of pineapple around the rim of a tall cocktail glass. Dip the glass in the coconut blossom nectar.

Blitz the pineapple, lemon juice, coconut water kefir, coconut yogurt, coconut milk and ice cubes in a blender until creamy and frothy.

Pour immediately into the prepared glass. Garnish the rim with the pineapple wedge and pop in the leaf (if using) and two straws.

PINE POLLEN AND POMEGRANATE MIMOSA

This bright Parisian cocktail is titled after the more common name for the bright yellow flowering *Acacia dealbata* plant. Native to Australia, the plant was introduced to the South of France in the nineteenth century by wealthy English with homes on the gorgeous Côte d'Azur. The beautifully scented mimosa plant now grows prolifically in the south of France from Bormes-les-Mimosas to the perfume capital Grasse, and you'll see it at its best in bloom from January to March. We can't wait to go back and check it out on a (strictly business) research trip really soon.

In the meantime, we've added pine pollen for a hit of sunless vitamin D3, plus clementine, a dash of pomegranate molasses and alcohol-free sparkling wine.

PREP   5 minutes
SERVES   5

50ml (2fl oz) pomegranate
  molasses (available
  at most supermarkets
  and health food stores)
350ml (12fl oz)
  clementine juice
3 teaspoons pine pollen
  (available online and in
  some health food stores)
ice cubes
750ml (1⅓ pints) sparkling
  alcohol-free wine, chilled

TO GARNISH
pomegranate seeds

Pour the pomegranate molasses, clementine juice and pine pollen into a cocktail shaker filled with ice, and shake until emulsified.

Divide the sunny liquid between five champagne flutes. Top with chilled sparkling alcohol-free wine and garnish with the jewels of pomegranate.

Vive La Révolution!

VIRGIN DAIQUIRI
(STRAWBERRY AND MANGO)

This virgin strawberry daiquiri is a favourite of ours – Andrea loves it because it is SO fruity and SO cool and SO easy. Catherine loves it because the colour reminds her of 17 years at Virgin. Ha! Not really!

We wish we could make this sound more skilful, but really it's literally just tossing the ingredients in a blender and blending until smooth and frosty. So, if you are like Catherine, prone to disaster in the kitchen, this one's a safe bet for you.

PREP   15 minutes
SERVES   2

PART ONE
300g (10½ oz) frozen
 strawberries
60ml (4 tablespoons)
 freshly squeezed
 lime juice
120ml (4fl oz) Coconut
 Water Kefir (see
 page 25)

PART TWO
1 large mango, peeled,
 cubed and frozen
30ml (2 tablespoons)
 freshly squeezed
 lime juice
30ml (2 tablespoons)
 Coconut Water Kefir
 (see page 25)

TO GARNISH
lime slices
fresh strawberries

OK, there is a tiny bit of method required; this cocktail requires 2 blending processes – and speed.

Put the frozen strawberries, lime juice and coconut water kefir in a blender. Blitz until smooth.

Divide the strawberry mix between two chilled hurricane glasses.

Rinse the blender, then add the frozen mango, lime juice and coconut water kefir and blitz until smooth.

Spoon the mango daiquiri over the strawberry.

Garnish with lime slices and strawberries.

CHOOSE LIFE PARTY PUNCH

Club Tropicana, drinks are free – from alcohol and sugar! Let's get on our party whites and neon accessories and turn up the '80s disco… This is a big bright punch which works brilliantly for a barbecue or pool party. You can create a punch bowl from the watermelon shell itself, hollowed out. All you need to do is add some multicoloured straws (non-plastic of course) and let everyone get involved.

PREP   20 minutes
SERVES   20

1 large watermelon,
    weighing approx 4kg
    (9lb), chilled
ice cubes
500ml (18fl oz) Coconut
    Water Kefir (see page
    25)
100ml (3½ fl oz) freshly
    squeezed lime juice
750ml (1¹/₃ pints) sparkling
    mineral water, chilled

TO GARNISH
mint sprigs
slices of lime

Slice off the top of the watermelon using a sharp knife. Regardless of what else happens at the party, it is best to be sober at this point. Scoop out the flesh of the watermelon until the rind is left with minimal pink showing. Reserve the hollowed-out watermelon shell to use as a bowl.

Purée the watermelon flesh, in batches, in a blender or food processor. Strain through a fine-mesh sieve into a bowl, and discard the solids. You will be left with about 2 litres (3½ pints) of watermelon juice.

If you're preparing in advance, then at this stage you can store the watermelon juice in the fridge for a few hours to keep it very chilled until you are ready to serve.

To serve, put ice cubes into the watermelon punch bowl and pour in the chilled watermelon juice. Add the coconut water kefir, lime juice and sparkling mineral water. Stir to combine. Garnish with mint sprigs and lime slices.

3

MARTINIS

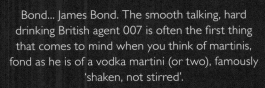

Bond... James Bond. The smooth talking, hard drinking British agent 007 is often the first thing that comes to mind when you think of martinis, fond as he is of a vodka martini (or two), famously 'shaken, not stirred'.

If Ian Fleming was writing today, we'd like to think that he'd have an exotic double agent seducing Bond over a Lychee and Yuzu martini (see page 46) with the new promise: 'Shaken, not slurred.'

LYCHEE AND YUZU MARTINI

The best place to experience a fresh lychee is in Southeast Asia where, at their peak of ripeness, they have developed perfumed exquisite flavours of roses, pineapples, green grapes and even marzipan. Try to avoid the canned versions as they are always in sugary syrup – wait for nature to present them fresh in the summer.

In China and Japan, the citrus fruit yuzu is prized for enhancing drinks and sauces. Just the scent of yuzu is said to be able to alleviate negative emotional stress, tension and mild anxiety. A Zen bar ingredient for when you're under pressure to bang out those cocktails for early party guests.

PREP   5 minutes
SERVES   2

6 fresh lychees, peeled and
   stoned, plus 2 for garnish
½ teaspoon yuzu juice
8 fresh mint leaves
1 teaspoon peeled and
   chopped fresh ginger
250ml (9fl oz) coconut
   water
6 ice cubes

Put the lychees, yuzu juice, mint and ginger in a cocktail shaker and press all the ingredients together with a muddler. Continue to mash until the lychees are broken down.

Add the coconut water and ice cubes to the shaker and shake vigorously.

Strain into two chilled martini glasses and garnish with a whole lychee.

COSMOPOLITAN
(AKA CRANTINI)

Miranda asked Carrie, 'Why did we stop drinking cosmos?' and Carrie replied, 'Because everyone else started.' The cosmo peaked as the most sophisticated New York accessory during the height of *Sex and The City* fame, we all drank millions of them, then they fell out of favour – probably after seeing the wrong end of one too many hen nights. Here we share a very quick and easy cosmopolitan in our typical Redemption style: all the fuss and pizzazz; none of the bad stuff.

PREP   5 minutes

SERVES   1

50ml (2fl oz) cranberry juice

4 teaspoons freshly squeezed orange juice

4 teaspoons freshly squeezed lemon juice

4 teaspoons Birch Syrup (see below)

100ml (3½fl oz)coconut water

ice

TO GARNISH

edible flowers

Pour all the ingredients into a cocktail shaker half filled with ice cubes. Shake vigorously and strain into a chilled martini glass.

Garnish with edible flowers because life is too short to be burning orange rind. Drink wearing heels without fear of falling over.

BIRCH SYRUP

MAKES   900ml

This is the equivalent to a simple sugar syrup or gomme, which is used the world over to sweeten cocktails. We use xylitol and water to make ours and the results taste the same.

Place 500g (17½oz) xylitol (see page 12) and 500ml (18fl oz) filtered water or mineral water in a small saucepan over a medium heat. Stir occasionally until the xylitol has fully dissolved.

Cool slightly, then pour into a sterilised bottle (see page 16) and store in the fridge for up to a month.

SNICKERTINI

There's a part of all of us that wants to gorge on creamy, sugary things without caring about the consequences. At Redemption, we try to invent things that trick that naughty part of you into thinking you have been sated but instead we're delivering a nutritional punch. Here we have Peruvian maca mixed with pure vanilla, which has a distinct malt-like flavour. Add to that nature's own caramel king, the Medjool date, with a hit of antioxidant-rich raw cacao, plus a peanutty protein bite. It's a fantastically indulgent creation – which we have brought right back down to earth by naming it after the Snickers bar. Just so you *think* you're having something bad.

PREP 10 minutes
SERVES 2

375ml (13fl oz) cold
   coconut milk
2 tablespoons peanut
   butter powder
4 Medjool dates
2 tablespoons raw cacao
   powder, plus extra to
   sprinkle
1 tablespoon maca powder
½ teaspoon pure vanilla
   extract
4–6 ice cubes

Combine all of the ingredients, except the ice cubes, in a high-speed blender and blitz until the dates are completely broken down and the liquid is smooth. Now add the ice and blend again to create a thicker shake that's cold and creamy.

Pour into two chilled champagne coupes and shake a little raw cacao on the top. Serve immediately.

Note

MACA is a vegetable root from Peru that is a superfood aphrodisiac, increasing your sex drive, improving energy and stamina and boosting fertility. So make sure you serve the Snickertini to the stud in your life.

ESPRESSO REMOLACHA

The espresso martini was invented by a famous barman, the late Dick Bradsell, in Soho in the late '80s. It's said he created it to please a model when she asked for something to 'Wake me up, then f**k me up.' Being Redemption, our take on it obviously only does the former! We like the bitter combination of coffee and super-healthy beetroot juice, balanced by the maple syrup. If you have been overindulging, it's a great hangover cure.

PREP   5 minutes
SERVES 2

6 ice cubes
50ml (2fl oz) espresso (or
    just really strong coffee)
300ml (½ pint) cold-
    pressed beetroot juice
2 tablespoons maple syrup

TO GARNISH
6 coffee beans

Put the ice cubes in a cocktail shaker and add the coffee, beetroot juice and maple syrup. Shake vigorously.

Pour into two chilled martini glasses. Garnish each with a few coffee beans and don't forget to smile.

Note

BEETROOT JUICE is a great antioxidant with a myriad of health benefits – it detoxifies the liver, lowers blood pressure and improves blood flow, which is great for overall heart health. We can't promise it will mend a broken heart, but it's great for the rare (ahem) occasion on which you may have overindulged.

FLU FIGHTERS MARTINI

ANDREA My stepdaughter, the lovely Alice, worked with us in the early days of Redemption and this is her invention. An ailing customer asked her to make a cocktail that had every flu-busting ingredient she could find in the bar. Of course she obliged, and the result happened to be delicious! It has been modified a little over the years, but at its heart it is a hot, feisty little number, which is why we named it in homage to the rock band.

PREP   10 minutes
SERVES   1

80ml (3½fl oz) coconut
   water
50ml (2fl oz) freshly
   squeezed orange juice
1 tablespoon freshly
   squeezed lemon juice
1 tablespoon freshly
   squeezed lime juice
4 teaspoons Rhubarb
   Cordial (see page 30),
   or elderflower cordial,
   shop-bought if you prefer
4 teaspoons pure aloe
   vera juice
1cm (½ in) piece fresh ginger,
   peeled
1cm (½ in) slice red chilli
a couple of ice cubes

TO GARNISH
slices of ginger and
   a chilli, to garnish

Put all the ingredients, except the ice cubes, in a blender and blitz well.

If you wish, you can pass the blended liquid through a fine-mesh sieve for an elegantly smooth drink. It is equally delicious and slightly spicier not passed, with the chilli flecks remaining, so it's entirely up to you whether you follow this step or not.

Put the ice cubes in a cocktail shaker and pour over the elixir. Shake well to chill and pour into a large chilled martini glass.

Garnish with a slice of fresh ginger and a chilli.

Notes

CHILLI contains up to seven times the vitamin C levels of an orange and has properties for fighting sinus congestion.

GINGER ROOT has long been used in traditional alternative medicine. It is a great aid to digestion, reduces nausea and helps the body to fight off the flu virus and common colds.

ALOE VERA JUICE is packed with vitamins, including B, C and E, as well as folic acid, all of which fortify the body's immune system.

CINDERELLA

MARTINIS

Like Cinderella's show-stopping ballgown, this drink can be made with a couple of flicks of your magic wand (your blender) – and you will dazzle the crowd. The only caveat is that unless you have a real-life fairy godmother to whisk up all the ferments, cordials and shrubs you require, you'll need to keep your rags on and get busy shrubbing in the cellar before your moment of glory.

The traditional Cinderella is an easy mix of three juices, grenadine and ginger ale, but we thought that was too ordinary so ours uses tepache, ginger switchel and homemade grenadine. And being alcohol-free, you definitely *shall not* lose your shoe at midnight.

PREP   5 minutes
SERVES   2

4 tablespoons Quick
  Gingered Tepache
  (see page 32)
4 tablespoons freshly
  squeezed lemon juice
4 tablespoons freshly
  squeezed orange juice
2 tablespoons Maple
  and Ginger Switchel
  (see page 21)
100ml (3½fl oz) sparkling
  mineral water
2 tablespoons Grenadine
  (see page 22)

TO GARNISH
edible organic flowers
  and petals
Hibiscus Flower Dust
  (see right)

Pour the tepache, juices, switchel, sparkling water and grenadine into a blender and blitz until frothy.

Pour into chilled hollow-stemmed champagne coupes.

Garnish with flowers and sprinkle with a little hibiscus dust.

HIBISCUS FLOWER DUST

MAKES 150g

Dried hibiscus flowers make wonderful decorations, and the deep red colour and tart taste work well mixed with xylitol to garnish drinks, the rims of glasses and even cakes and cookies. Ground dried hibiscus flowers mixed with fine Himalayan salt can also make a great finishing touch to savoury dishes.

You'll need 50g of dried hibiscus flowers – you can buy these online whole or ground. If you buy whole flowers, grind them to a fine dust. Mix this with 100g xylitol (see page 12), then sieve. Store in a clean, dry airtight jar for up to a year.

PIROUETTE

As Einstein said, 'We dance for laughter, we dance for tears, we dance for madness, we dance for fears, we dance for hopes, we dance for screams, we are the dancers, we create the dreams.'

Most of us have got a little bit of ballerina inside of us and with this elegant drink you can swirl and spin around the room spreading magic and sparkle, but with none of the dizziness (and less chance of face planting).

PREP   5 minutes
SERVES 2

50ml (2fl oz) Juniper Syrup
  (see below)
150ml (¼ pint) birch water
  (available from health
  food stores and some
  supermarkets)
5 teaspoons freshly
  squeezed lemon juice
100ml (3½fl oz) pressed
  pink lady apple juice
5 teaspoons Grenadine
  (see page 22)
1 cube of frozen aquafaba
  (see page 12)

TO GARNISH
edible flower petals,
  such as organic pink
  rose petals

Put all the ingredients in a blender and blitz together until pink and frothy.

Alternatively, you can use 2 cubes of aquafaba rather than one, put all the ingredients in a cocktail shaker and shake vigorously while performing one perfect pirouette.

Strain into two chilled champagne coupes. Garnish with pink petals and drink immediately.

JUNIPER SYRUP

MAKES **500 ML (18FL OZ)**

Muddle 6 tablespoons juniper berries, 1 tablespoon coriander seeds and 1 tablespoon cardamom pods in a saucepan until they've all just cracked open a little. Pare off thin strips of the peel of 1 lemon and 1 orange, and add to the saucepan.

Add 1 teaspoon angelica, 50g (1¾oz) xylitol and 500ml (18fl oz) birch water. Bring to the boil then simmer for 10 minutes. Pour into a clean jar and cool.

Steep the mixture in the jar, covered, in the fridge overnight. Strain through a small sieve into a sterilised bottle (see page 12) and keep refrigerated for up to 2 weeks.

4

MOJITOS

The modern mojito is a far cry from
concoction dished out in the 1500s to Sir
Drake's scurvy-ridden crew in Cuba. T
burly sailors recovered by drinking a to
aguardiente de caña (a rough local alcoho
lime juice, mint and sugar cane. Not long
drink named El Draque became popular i

While we can't claim to have cured scurv
any of our mojitos, we can guarantee tha
will lift your spirits and put a spring in yo
without leaving you 'three sheets to the

BASIL AND
BLACKBERRY BRAMBLE

The bramble is one of the many cocktails created by the legendary British bartender and father of modern cocktail culture, Dick Bradsell. We loved Dick for, amongst other things, advocating the use of proper fresh fruit juice in cocktails and also for creating the modern classic espresso martini (see our version, the Espresso Remolacha on page 51).

We'd like to think that if Dick was still alive today he would celebrate the recent innovation in quality non-alcoholic cocktails, and that he would champion us at Redemption as he did for so many others in our industry. We wanted to make an alcohol-free bramble in homage to Dick but we couldn't get it to sing until we experimented with muddling in fresh basil with blackberry, and now it works like magic.

PREP   5 minutes
SERVES   2

6 plump blackberries,
  plus 6 to serve
6 purple basil leaves,
  torn juice of I lemon
100ml (3½fl oz) Maple
  and Ginger Switchel (see
  page 21)
ice cubes
crushed ice
chilled sparkling
  mineral water

TO GARNISH
purple basil stems
lemon peel twists

Put the 6 blackberries, basil leaves, lemon juice and switchel in a cocktail shaker and muddle until the blackberries have broken down.

Half-fill the shaker with ice cubes and shake well.

Half-fill two chilled highball glasses with crushed ice and strain over the bramble.

Top with sparkling mineral water.

Garnish each glass with extra blackberries, plus a purple basil stem and a lemon peel twist.

ALOHA

Aloha is a lovely word; it's used as a greeting, of course, but it's also full of good intentions and feelings, meaning love, affection, kindness and goodness. We can't think of anything better to celebrate our philosophy at Redemption in general, and this fruity concoction specifically.

Hawaii was once the big kahuna in pineapple production and many recipes using the fruit come from these islands. Instead of pineapple juice we've used our fermented pineapple tepache to give it a modern, global Redemption twist.

PREP   5 minutes
SERVES   2

8 fresh mint leaves
1 lime, cut into wedges
crushed ice
50ml (2fl oz) freshly
  squeezed
  lime juice
50ml (2fl oz) passion fruit
  pulp
300ml (½ pint) Quick
  Gingered Tepache (see
  page 32)

TO GARNISH
pineapple leaves
lime wheels
Hibiscus Flower Dust
  (see page 56)

Muddle the mint leaves with the lime wedges and juice in the bottom of two large highball glasses.

Half-fill the glasses with crushed ice, then stir well to blend all the ingredients together.

Add the passion fruit pulp then stir. Top up with chilled tepache.

Garnish each glass with a pineapple leaf, lime wheel and a dusting of hibiscus flower dust.

MY THAI

What a fantastically beautiful and charming country Thailand is, the jewel of the crown of planet Earth. We both travelled the country extensively when we were young and carefree – hopefully we will have the chance to do the same again when our working days are over. We drank something similar to this at the Full Moon parties, but with a large dose of *mehkong* (a potent local rice spirit). If you don't want the room to spin as fast as the ceiling fan, try our vibrant alcohol-free adaptation.

PREP   5 minutes
SERVES   2

6 fresh mint leaves
6 Thai sweet basil leaves
100ml (3½fl oz)
   Lemongrass and Chilli
   Shrub (see page 20)
50ml (2fl oz) freshly
   squeezed lime juice
ice cubes
crushed ice
1 lime, cut into thin slices
300ml (½ pint) chilled
   sparkling mineral water

TO GARNISH
4 fresh mint leaves
2 Thai sweet basil leaves
little Thai chillies
lemongrass stalks
   (optional)

Muddle the mint leaves, Thai sweet basil leaves and the lemongrass and chilli shrub in a cocktail shaker. Add the lime juice and ice cubes and shake for a few seconds.

Half-fill two Collins glasses with crushed ice and lime slices.

Strain the shaken drink into the prepared glasses and top with sparkling mineral water.

Garnish with mint, sweet basil, Thai chillies and lemongrass stalks, if using.

APPLE MOCKJITO

Who doesn't love a mojito? It has been popular in Cuba for centuries and became really fashionable in the world's best bars from LA to London to Sydney since the '90s. In our sugar-free, alcohol-free version, we've not only managed to keep the balance of flavours as exciting as the original, but it's supremely thirst-quenching. In fact, it has the ability to make you feel like you've had a power shower, washed your hair AND changed your outfit. Perfect for rejuvenating during long summer afternoons.

PREP   5 minutes
SERVES   1

6 fresh mint leaves
4 lime wedges
20ml (4 teaspoons) freshly
   squeezed lime juice
25ml (5 teaspoons)
   organic cold-pressed
   apple juice
½ teaspoon coconut sugar
crushed ice
150ml (¼ pint) chilled
   sparkling mineral water

TO GARNISH
long mint stem
dusting of coconut sugar
thin slice of Granny Smith
   apple, dipped in lime juice

Muddle the mint leaves with the lime wedges, lime juice, apple juice and sugar in the bottom of a large highball glass.

Add enough ice to fill just over half the glass, then stir well to blend all the ingredients together.

Top up with sparkling mineral water.

Garnish with an extra long mint stem, a dusting of coconut sugar and a slice of apple.

RHUBARB AND GINGER SPRITZER

CATHERINE Sundays were the busiest day at the vicarage where I grew up, with church in the morning and the evening. Mum somehow managed to find the time to rustle up a rhubarb and ginger crumble which used to magically appear after she'd served lunch for the family, plus guests from the congregation. She never showed us how she did it. She must have sneaked out at midnight on Saturday to pick the prolific rhubarb from the garden. This spritzer is a lovely, healthy homage to my mum, Pauline – and to all mums who work miracles.

PREP   5 minutes
SERVES   2

10 fresh mint leaves
150ml (¼ pint) Rhubarb
   Cordial (see page 30)
50ml (2fl oz) freshly
   squeezed lemon juice
50ml (2fl oz) Maple and
   Ginger Switchel (see
   page 21)
200ml (7fl oz) sparkling
   mineral water
crushed ice

TO GARNISH
transparently thin
   ribbons of rhubarb,
   peeled with a swivel-
   head vegetable peeler

Blitz the mint leaves, rhubarb cordial, lemon juice and switchel in a blender.

Half-fill two chilled highball glasses with crushed ice and ribbons of rhubarb.

Pour the rhubarb, ginger and mint mixture over the ice, top with chilled sparkling water and serve.

5

LONG DRINKS

Cocktails can be labour intensive and while your guests will undoubtedly appreciate the time and effort you've spent on your creations, at a certain point in the event you may want to relax and enjoy yourself too. That's when you turn to this section, in particular the Lemongrass Lemonade (page 72) and the Hibiscus Ice Tea (page 77) as both can be made in large jugs and left next to a bucket of ice and a stack of glasses – it's time to serve yourselves, my friends, my shift at the bar is over!

LEMONGRASS LEMONADE

'If life gives you lemons, make lemonade,' as the saying goes. But what do you do when life gives you lemongrass? We say you rejoice, give thanks to Mother Earth, pair it with some lemons, concoct this vibrant smasher of a drink, and blow all the other kiddy entrepreneurs with their lemonade stalls *right* out of the water.

LONG DRINKS

PREP	10 minutes
COOK	60 minutes
	+ overnight
	steeping
MAKES	750ml (1⅓ pints)

6 lemongrass stalks,
  roughly chopped
1.5 litres (2¾ pints) still
  mineral water
150g (5½oz) coconut sugar
4 large limes, peeled with
  a swivel-head vegetable
  peeler, then juiced
crushed ice

TO GARNISH
pink peppercorns
lemongrass stalks

Place the lemongrass and measured water in a large saucepan over a medium heat. Bring to a rolling boil, then reduce to a simmer for 60 minutes.

Remove from the heat, and add the coconut sugar, lime juice and lime peel. Stir well, then leave to cool.

Cover and put in the fridge overnight to steep.

The next day, strain the lemonade into a jug or bottle and keep refrigerated.

To serve, pour into large copa or balloon glasses with plenty of crushed ice, garnished with pink peppercorns and lemongrass stalks.

MOSCOW MULE

Nobody knows why this drink is named after Moscow; it has nothing to do with Russia at all! It was invented from leftover stock of vodka and ginger beer in 1940s Manhattan, and later caught on in LA. It has always been served in a copper mug, which we love because not only does it look beautiful, it also keeps the cocktail cold for a long time as you sip it on a hot'n'steamy summer night in the city. We create the heat you'd get from vodka with the fresh ginger in the switchel.

PREP   5 minutes
SERVES   2

150ml (¼ pint) Maple and
   Ginger Switchel (see
   page 21)
100ml (3½fl oz) freshly
   squeezed lime juice
200ml (7fl oz) chilled
   sparkling mineral water
crushed ice

TO GARNISH
lime wedges and fresh mint

Put the switchel, lime juice and sparkling water in a jug and mix well.

Half-fill two copper mugs or Collins glasses with crushed ice. Pour over the ginger and lime concoction and garnish with lime wedges and fresh mint.

HIBISCUS ICED TEA

We created our signature iced tea by mistake… we are always making tea, only to get too busy in the restaurant to drink it while hot. So then we take our cold tea, add something from the bar – ginger, fresh herbs such as rosemary or mint, a cordial for sweetness, maybe a juice. Herbal teas (such as lemon balm or mint) or fruit teas work well and contain no caffeine, but if you do need that caffeine hit, this is overall the best combination we've come up with.

PREP   5 minutes
MAKES   1.2 litres

4 white tea bags
1 litre (1¾ pints) filtered
   or mineral water, just
   boiled
200ml (7fl oz) Hibiscus
   Cordial (see page 16)
50ml (2fl oz) freshly
   squeezed
   lime juice
½ teaspoon orange
   blossom water
½ teaspoon pure rose
   water
ice cubes

TO GARNISH
lemon or lime slices
orange blossoms or
   Hibiscus Flowers in
   Syrup (see page 17)

Steep the white tea bags in the just-boiled water for 10 minutes, then remove the tea bags. Let the infusion cool, then chill.

Add the hibiscus cordial, lime juice, orange blossom water and rose water, and stir.

Serve as a long drink with lots of ice, slices of lemon or lime and a blossom or two.

SHOREDITCH SUNRISE

The sun rises in the East, casting its iridescent hues of bright oranges and pinks over London's most exciting neighbourhood. The sins of the night before are (almost) forgotten as techies rise and shine to create the new economy. New artworks, neon signs, graffiti, tattoos and piercings appear magically overnight. People #needRedemption and get photographed in front of our angel wings to show they've been. We love our little corner of Shoreditch and the community we share it with. Here is our homage to our spiritual home.

PREP   5 minutes
SERVES 1

crushed ice
½ teaspoon orange
  blossom water
60ml (2fl oz) fresh blood
  orange juice
80ml (2½fl oz) fresh
  pineapple juice
4 teaspoons Maple
  and Ginger Switchel
  (see page 21)
30ml (1fl oz) Grenadine
  (see page 22)

TO GARNISH (choose one
  or some of the following)
pineapple wedge
cherries (if in season)
hibiscus flower
blood orange slice
cocktail umbrella
  (optional, but why not?!)

Fill a hurricane glass with crushed ice.

Pour over the orange blossom water, blood orange juice, pineapple juice and the switchel and swizzle.

Add the grenadine (which hopefully will sink to the bottom, then rise like a phoenix to the top).

Choose your garnish and serve immediately.

LOVE AND PEAS

From the delicateness of pea shoot tendrils, to the crunchy tender whole pods and the little sweet green pearls inside, it's amazing to think that you can eat the whole pea plant from root to shoot. We raise our own micro pea shoots in our restaurants – it's beautiful to see nature unfurling before us, allowing us all to take a moment to reflect at the wonder of it all. Love and peas, peas and love.

PREP   5 minutes
SERVES   2

large handful of pea
    shoot tendrils
100ml (3½fl oz) cucumber
    juice or approx. ½
    cucumber, peeled
    (reserve the peel)
4 large mint leaves
30ml (1fl oz) freshly
    squeezed lemon juice
pinch of Himalayan salt
160ml (5½fl oz) chilled
    fizzy rosemary water
    (see below)
1 teaspoon aquafaba
    (see page 12)
3 ice cubes

TO GARNISH
cucumber peel
2 bamboo skewers
pea shoot tendrils

Simply put all the ingredients in a blender and blitz.

Pour into two very chilled champagne coupes.

To create the garnishes, roll a length of cucumber peel up with the dark green on the outside, and thread onto one end of a bamboo skewer. Rest this across the glass and top with a pea shoot tendril. Repeat for the other glass.

Tip

ROSEMARY WATER is a relatively new sparkling drink on the market and is quite wonderful, but you can make it yourself either by adding a few drops of food-grade pure rosemary essence to sparkling water or by the slightly lengthier infusion method (bruise fresh rosemary and steep in sparkling mineral water for 48 hours to impart the delicate oils).

6

FIZZ

'Get busy with the fizzy!' Anyone growing up in the '70s or '80s will remember the joy of the Sodastream, when making fizzy drinks at home was just about the coolest thing ever.

Drinks that fizz and bubble are often drunk as part of celebrations, the effervescent exuberance in the glass reflected on the faces of the guests, sparkling dialogue and a general buzz. The fizz provides a real sense of occasion.

ROSEMARY AND POMEGRANATE FIZZ

Get seriously loved up with this romantic combination of pomegranate, a symbol of fertility and abundance, and fragrant rosemary, which has traditionally been used to represent marriage. Conscious coupling in a glass!

COOK	10 minutes
	+ cooling time
PREP	5 minutes
SERVES	8

400ml (14fl oz)
  pomegranate juice
4 sprigs rosemary
juice of ½ lemon
750ml (1⅓ pints) alcohol-
  free sparkling wine,
  chilled

TO GARNISH
pomegranate seeds
flowering rosemary sprigs

Pour the pomegranate juice into a small saucepan. Lightly bruise the rosemary by rubbing it between your fingers, and add it to the pan. Bring to the boil and reduce for 10 minutes, then add the lemon juice.

Leave to cool, then strain and chill until ready to use.

Pour 30ml of the rosemary and pomegranate mixture into each champagne flute and top up with alcohol-free sparkling wine.

Garnish each glass with a few pomegranate jewels and a rosemary sprig.

BLACK MAGIC

What black magic is this… a detox cocktail? That's an oxymoron, surely?

This impressive concoction is made with fresh lemons for a vitamin C and potassium kick, activated charcoal for its detoxifying properties, and cayenne pepper, which adds a stimulatory heating effect. All three ingredients aid the metabolism, and the body's cleansing and elimination process.

It's important to select activated charcoal made from coconut shells or other natural sources, not just a lump from your barbecue. Activated charcoal is popular medically for a safe and effective treatment of poisoning and drug overdoses. It's used to reduce bloating and gas and even prevent hangovers, so a glass of Black Magic is perfect for any of your guests who arrive 'hanging like a loose tooth' from the night before.

PREP   5 minutes
SERVES   2

300ml (½ pints) sparkling
  mineral water
juice of 2 lemons
  (you need 120ml/4fl oz)
¼ teaspoon activated
  black charcoal (available in
  health stores and online)
2 tablespoons maple syrup
pinch of cayenne pepper
1 frozen cube of aquafaba
  (see page 12)
Hibiscus Flower Dust (see
  page 56), optional, to
  serve

Simply blitz all the ingredients in a blender until frothy, and pour into two chilled martini glasses.

There should be a lovely creamy foam sitting on top of the dark magic below. Garnish with Hibiscus Flower Dust, if using, and serve.

Note

ACTIVATED CHARCOAL, with its porous negatively charged surface of micro nooks and crannies, grabs and locks in the positive charged toxins and gas and sweeps them away.

BOLLYWOOD

We often look to India for inspiration, including for food and drinks. Nowhere else has India's perfect combination of ancient, holistic and healing wisdom, wrapped up in exotic and vibrant explosions of colour, texture and artistry. This bright neon number will certainly be on the menu when we launch Redemption Goa.

PREP	30 minutes
COOK	10 minutes
SERVES	2

6 green cardamom pods
 (see note)
ice cubes
5 teaspoons mango purée
5 teaspoons fresh turmeric
 juice (see note)
5 teaspoons freshly
 squeezed lime juice
50ml (2fl oz) Maple and
 Ginger Switchel (see
 page 21)
200ml (7fl oz) sparkling
 mineral water

TO GARNISH
edible flowers

Bruise the cardamom pods (bash with a wooden spoon) to release the aroma.

Pour into the bottom of two tall flutes and top with sparkling mineral water.

Garnish in true Bollywood style with brightly coloured flowers.

FIZZ

Notes

TURMERIC JUICE can be bought in little shot bottles at health food stores and some supermarkets. At Redemption, we make our own using fresh turmeric roots washed and blended with mineral water, which we then strain through a fine sieve. WARNING – turmeric stains very badly, so watch your hands and your clothes! It will also stain the blender and sieve.

GREEN CARDAMOM is harvested earlier than black cardamom and has more citrusy aromas – as it gets riper, the cardamom develops a more smoky flavour. Cardamom is one of the core spices revered in the practice of Ayurveda (ancient Indian medicine), used in cooking to aid digestion and detoxification. Its strong aromatic flavour pairs well with turmeric and mango in this recipe. Cardamom is familiar to many as it is the prominent spice flavour in Masala Chai.

PEACH AND PASSION BELLINI

A twist on the classic Bellini, this peach and passion fruit sorbet cocktail makes an elegant alcohol-free alternative for celebrations, with very little fuss once the sorbet is made. It's romantic as hell but don't push your luck drinking one of these on a gondola ride in Venice. Even though it's alcohol-free, your trip might be less peachy and passionate if the frozen sorbet ends up in your lover's lap.

PREP	40 minutes
COOK	10 minutes
FREEZE	10 hours
SERVES	7–8

FOR THE SORBET
300g (10½oz) xylitol (see page 12)
300ml (½ pint) filtered water
1 unwaxed lemon, sliced
500g (1lb 2oz) peach halves, stoned
seeds and pulp from 4 passion fruits

TO SERVE
750ml (1⅓ pints) alcohol-free sparkling wine, chilled
seeds from 1 passion fruit
edible flowers (optional)

Begin by making the sorbet. Combine the xylitol, measured water and lemon slices in a saucepan over a low heat. Bring to the boil while stirring until the xylitol dissolves.

Add the peaches and passion fruit pulp and seeds. Simmer for 10 minutes then remove from the heat and cool for 30 minutes.

Lift out the peach halves, reserving the passion fruit syrup but discarding the lemon slices. Allow to cool.

Strain the passion syrup through a sieve and push through as much of the pulp as possible without breaking the seeds.

Peel and discard the skins of the cooled peaches.

Blitz the strained syrup and peaches in a blender or food processor.

Pour the mixture into a large freezerproof container so the sorbet mix forms a thin layer.

Cover and place in the freezer for 6 hours until firm.

Break up the sorbet with a heavy metal spoon, then transfer to a food processor and process until a smooth frozen purée forms.

Put into a deep freezerproof container and freeze for a minimum of 3 hours or until the sorbet is firm.

When you're ready to serve, scoop the sorbet into small balls and place on a tray in the freezer for a minimum of 1 hour to refreeze hard.

Chill the champagne coupes well. Pop a scoop of sorbet into each glass and top up with alcohol-free sparkling wine.

Garnish each drink with a few passion fruit seeds and edible flowers if using.

BLOOD ORANGE, BASIL
AND THYME KOMBUCHA

The combination here of blood orange zest, basil leaves and lemon thyme is pure alchemy. Although we include the recipe for making kombucha (see page 27) you can cheat and make this aromatic bitters cocktail using store-bought hooch if time is of the essence. The results will be quite different, but still delicious.

THE SLOW METHOD WITH YOUR OWN KOMBUCHA:

PREP   10 minutes
FERMENT 48 hours
MAKES   1 litre (1¾ pints)

peel of 1 blood orange –
  peel into thin strips
  using a zester
5 large basil leaves, torn
3 lemon thyme stalks
1 litre (1¾ pints)
  Kombucha (see page 27)

TO GARNISH
lemon thyme flowers

Simply put all the ingredients in a sterilised jar or bottle (see page 16) and seal tightly.

Store at room temperature for 48 hours.

The pressure will build up quickly if it is warm and to avoid explosions it is recommended that you 'burp' the bottle daily (remove the lid to release the gas).

Strain the finished fizz through either a nut bag or a very fine strainer into a bowl or jug. Decant into a clean bottle and keep in the fridge. Consume within 12 weeks.

To serve, pour into chilled champagne coupes and garnish with lemon thyme flowers.

WHEN YOU'RE SHORT ON TIME, USING BOUGHT KOMBUCHA:

PREP   5 minutes
SERVES 6

juice of 1 blood orange
3 basil leaves
750ml (1⅓ pints) plain
  sparkling kombucha,
  chilled

TO GARNISH
lemon thyme stalks

Blitz all the ingredients in a blender, then pour through a fine-mesh strainer.

Pour into chilled glasses and garnish each with a lemon thyme stalk.

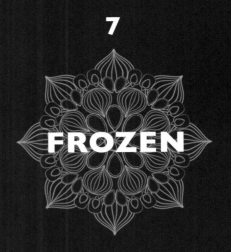

7

FROZEN

Summer slush puppies, bright blue and frosty drinks... the child inside us loves the idea of them, but they are loaded with refined sugar, artificial flavours and colours, and really are devoid of any nutrition.

Good news... help is on the way! Pimp up your summer with nutritious delicious frozen fun.

FROZEN PINEAPPLE MARGARITA

The pineapple is such a favourite item of ours at Redemption that we bought an antique chandelier in its image. The uniquely beautiful, dramatic structure of this fruit contains such a delightful, bright sweet ooziness. In true Redemption style, you can drink several of these Frozen Pineapple Margaritas and you won't have to hide under your sombrero from the embarrassment of getting your maracas out last night.

PREP   15 minutes
SERVES 4

1kg (2lb 3oz) small
   pineapple chunks, frozen
250ml (9fl oz) Quick
   Gingered Tepache (see
   page 32)
juice of 4 fresh limes
¼ teaspoon Himalayan salt

FOR THE GARNISH
dried hibiscus flowers
Himalayan salt
1 lime, cut into wedges

Chill four margarita glasses in the freezer for at least 10 minutes.

Prepare the garnish by grinding together the dried hibiscus flowers and Himalayan salt and placing in a saucer or shallow dish. Set aside.

Put the frozen pineapple chunks, tepache, lime juice and Himalayan salt in a blender and blend until smooth.

Run a wedge of lime around the rim of each glass and then dip the rim into the hibiscus salt.

Scoop the frozen margarita into the glasses, being careful not to disturb the salty rim.

Optional: get your maracas out.

REDEMPTION ROYALE

Valentine's is our most popular night of the year at Redemption. Who knew sober dating would catch on in the UK? This romantic drink started out as a Valentine's special and quickly became one of our bestsellers all year round. Let's embrace conscious coupling!

PREP   10 minutes
SERVES   1

100ml (3½fl oz)
  pomegranate juice
6 large or 10 small
  frozen strawberries
2 ice cubes
50ml (2fl oz) Hibiscus
  Cordial (see page 16)
2 drops pure rose water
  (available in health food
  stores and online)

TO GARNISH
pomegranate seeds
edible flowers

Blitz all the ingredients in a blender.

Scoop the contents into a large martini glass.

Garnish with the pomegranate seeds and edible flowers.

FRED AND GINGER

Like Fred Astaire and Ginger Rogers, pear and ginger were made for each other.

The base of this drink is our attention-grabbing pear and ginger shrub, but with mellowing maple syrup to smooth things out and just a sprinkling of cinnamon to round off the relationship, we think this number will glide into your top ten.

PREP 5 minutes +
      freezing time
      for pear cubes

SERVES 2–3

250g (9oz) frozen diced
  peeled pear
80ml (2½fl oz) Pear and
  Lemon Thyme Shrub
  (see page 18)
25ml (¾fl oz) Maple and
  Ginger Switchel (see
  page 21)
40ml (1½fl oz) maple
  syrup
½ teaspoon ground
  cinnamon
4 ice cubes

TO GARNISH
edible flowers
cinnamon sticks

Put all the ingredients into a blender and either turn on slowly or pulse.

Scoop into chilled Nick and Nora cocktail glasses.

Gently float a few edible flowers on top, add a cinnamon stick, face the music, and dance.

FROZEN

HORCHA-TA-TA

ANDREA I first discovered the rice-based, slightly sweet, creamy beverage known as horchata in Mexico, sold by street-food vendors along the Yucatán Peninsula, and then again in Venezuela. So I suppose I shouldn't have been surprised to find its origins are Spanish and the drink was brought to the Americas by homesick *conquistadors*. In Venezuela, a type of horchata called *chicha* is made with toasted sesame seeds. This gave me the idea to add tahini to our frozen version, which thickens and adds a caramel-like flavour.

PREP   15 minutes
SOAK   12 hours
SERVES   4

400ml (14fl oz) filtered
  water
225g (8oz) uncooked
  brown rice
4 tablespoons maple syrup
  (more if you like
  it sweeter)
400ml (14fl oz) rice cream
  (oat cream and coconut
  cream work well too)
2 teaspoons vanilla extract
1 teaspoon ground
  cinnamon
ice cubes
4 teaspoons tahini

TO GARNISH
cinnamon sticks

OPTIONAL
pecan crunch (see right)

Pour the water over the brown rice, stir, then cover and place in the fridge overnight.

The next day, remove from the fridge, transfer to a high-speed blender and blitz until smooth.

Strain the mixture through a nut bag into a bowl (a muslin or cheesecloth works equally well), squeezing to get every last drop out. Dispose of the pulp in your compost.

Stir in the maple syrup, rice cream, vanilla and cinnamon and return the horchata to the fridge. Keep it chilled until ready to serve; it will keep well in the fridge for 4 days.

When you're ready to serve, chill four margarita glasses in the freezer.

Measure the horchata and for every 200ml (7fl oz), blitz 4 cubes of ice and 1 teaspoon of tahini with the horchata until thick like a slushy. Scoop into the margarita glasses and garnish with a cinnamon stick and pecan crunch.

FOR THE PECAN CRUNCH

Preheat the oven to 200°C/400°F/gas mark 6 and line a baking tray with greaseproof paper. Mix 50g (1¾oz) pecan pieces with 2 tablespoons maple syrup. Rub with your hands to coat.

Spread the pecans in a single layer on the tray. Toast for 10 minutes, then allow to cool.

FRO-CO-RITA

CATHERINE The coco-rita was one of the first drinks we invented. We served it at our first pop up on a Hackney rooftop, back in the summer of 2013. It was our take on a margarita – except made with coconut water. Since then, we've moved on to making it frozen margarita style, and so the fro-co-rita was born. It is beautiful, simple and effective: the sourness comes from the lime and Himalayan rock salt, giving it that margarita bite. This is great as an apéritif, perfect for people who don't like sweet drinks, and it's also a good starter for someone who thinks drinking cocktails without alcohol is utter madness.

PREP   5 minutes
SERVES   1

50ml (2fl oz) coconut
  water
75ml (2½fl oz) lime juice
25ml (5 teaspoons)
  orange juice
50ml (2fl oz) Birch Syrup
  (see page 49)
ice cubes

TO GARNISH
Himalayan salt
lime wedge
pale edible flowers

Blitz the coconut water, lime juice, orange juice, Birch Syrup and ice cubes in a blender until the mixture resembles a sorbet.

Place the Himalayan salt in a saucer or shallow dish. Rub the rim of a chilled margarita glass with the lime wedge, and dip into the salt to make a salt rim.

Scoop out the fro-co-rita into the glass, towering up like Mont Blanc, then quickly garnish with the flowers and serve.

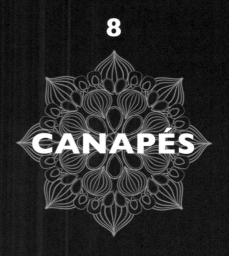

8

CANAPÉS

No party is complete without a food offering and canapés are the perfect partner for cocktails. Often people over cater and it's such a waste of your time and resources. Our rule of thumb when catering for events, and we've done many, is to allow 14–16 bites per person if canapés are being served instead of a main meal, or 8–10 bites if they are being served as nibbles at a cocktail party.

To make sure your canapés are a real hit, make sure they pack a flavour punch and look impossibly pretty.

SLOW-ROASTED
ACTIVATED ALMONDS

Almonds make a delicious and healthy snack, rich in vitamins and minerals, but to obtain their full nutritional potential they need to be activated. Like all nuts and seeds, a coat of indigestible phytates protects the almonds until conditions are right for germination. Soaking them in water activates the nuts from their dormant state and the phytate begins to break down, releasing the minerals to fuel the enzymes that the seed requires to grow into a new plant. After soaking our almonds overnight we flavour and gently dehydrate them (cooking them would kill the enzymes) to ensure all their nutritional content is available.

PREP	10 minutes
SOAK	12 hours
COOK	24 hours
MAKES	approx 1-litre (1¾-pint) jar

300g (7oz) raw almonds
still mineral water,
  to cover
2 teaspoons Himalayan salt
1 teaspoon smoked paprika
1 tablespoon nutritional
  yeast

Put the almonds, measured water and 1 teaspoon of Himalayan salt in a bowl. Cover and place in the fridge for 12 hours to soak.

Drain and rinse the nuts.

Mix the nuts in a bowl with the remaining Himalayan salt, smoked paprika and nutritional yeast.

Spread out on a baking tray lined with greaseproof paper and put into the oven on the lowest possible temperature (60°C/140°F/gas mark ¼) for 12–24 hours.

Cool and store in an airtight jar.

Tips

We recommend European almonds, especially Spanish.
This process works with other nuts – have a go with Brazil nuts, pecans or walnuts.

MINI SWEETCORN PANCAKES

ANDREA These mini sweetcorn pancakes served with scrumptious guacamole were a speciality of my mother's. I've altered her original recipe to make the pancakes vegan and gluten-free, but if anything they are actually crispier and tastier (sorry Mum!). These are really popular in our restaurants and when we serve them at top London fashion events.

PREP	20 minutes
COOK	10 minutes
MAKES	approx 30 canapés

275g (10oz) sweetcorn
  kernels
125ml (4fl oz) oat milk
½ teaspoon Himalayan salt
½ teaspoon cracked
  black pepper
bunch of spring onions,
  washed and sliced
bunch coriander, chopped
1 tablespoon white chia
  seeds, ground
½ red pepper, deseeded
  and diced small
30g (1oz) buckwheat flour
40g (1½oz) fine polenta
1 teaspoon baking powder
coconut oil or olive oil,
  for cooking
micro tomato halves, micro
  red amaranth or coriander
  leaves, to garnish

FOR THE GUACAMOLE
1 large ripe avocado, mashed
juice of 1 lime
½ chilli, deseeded
  and finely diced
¼ teaspoon Himalayan salt
¼ teaspoon black pepper

Put half of the sweetcorn and the oat milk, salt and pepper in a food processor and blitz until the kernels are puréed. Scrape into a mixing bowl. Mix the remaining sweetcorn kernels with half the spring onions, half the coriander and all other ingredients (except the oil) into the puréed corn, stirring until just combined.

Heat a little oil in a frying pan over a medium heat and drop 1 heaped teaspoon of mixture per pancake into the pan, trying to keep them perfectly round in shape.

Cook in batches, for 1–1½ minutes on each side, then transfer onto a tray. At this stage you can keep the pancakes covered in the fridge until the guests arrive, or even overnight.

To make the guacamole, combine all the ingredients along with the remaining coriander and spring onions and mix.

Preheat the oven to 240°C/475°F/gas mark 9.

Arrange the sweetcorn pancakes in a single layer on a baking tray and bake in the oven for 6–8 minutes until crispy and hot. Remove from the oven and use a palette knife to lift the pancakes onto a serving platter.

Dollop a teaspoon of guacamole on each pancake. Garnish with micro tomato halves, micro red amaranth or coriander leaves.

Serve at once – before they go out of fashion.

POLENTA FRIES WITH FERMENTED SMOKY KETCHUP

Easy peasy and kind of cheesy, baked polenta fries, deliciously crunchy on the outside and creamy on the inside. Serving with a bowl of fermented ketchup ups the health benefits tenfold. Thanks to our friend Chantal for the inspiration. The ketchup requires a 16-hour ferment and a couple of days to develop, so make sure you leave enough time.

PREP   10 minutes
COOK   40 minutes
SERVES   4 as nibbles

500ml (18fl oz) vegetable
  stock
2 tablespoons extra virgin
  olive oil
3 tablespoons nutritional
  yeast
1 unwaxed lemon, zested
½ teaspoon cayenne pepper
1 tablespoon maple syrup
½ teaspoon Himalayan salt
cracked pepper
160g (5½oz) fine polenta
extra virgin olive oil, for
  brushing the fries

FOR THE KETCHUP

MAKES   1.5 litres (2¾ pints)
FERMENT   16 hours

180ml (6fl oz) vegan
  Worcestershire sauce
125ml (4fl oz) raw apple
  cider vinegar
125ml (4fl oz) maple syrup
100ml 3½fl oz) Coconut
  Water Kefir (see page 25)
1 tablespoon smoked
  paprika
1 tablespoon Himalayan salt
1kg (2lb 3oz) organic
  tomato passata

First, make the ketchup. Combine the first six ketchup ingredients in a bowl and stir well. Add the tomato passata and stir again. Transfer to a large wide-necked glass or ceramic jar, place a clean thin cloth over the opening and secure with an elastic band. Leave for 16 hours to ferment in a warm place, the kitchen is ideal. Pour into sterilised bottles and cap or secure the jar with an airtight lid. Store in the fridge and allow the ketchup to develop for a couple of days.

To make the fries, put the stock, olive oil, nutritional yeast, lemon zest, cayenne, maple syrup, salt and pepper in a medium saucepan and bring to the boil.

Once it is boiling, slowly pour the polenta into the pan, stirring all the time – the mixture will end up being very thick. Pour the mix into a small square cake tin lined with non-stick baking parchment. Flatten and smooth the surface with the back of a large, wet spoon. Transfer to the fridge for an hour to cool and firm up.

Preheat the oven to 240°C/475°F/gas mark 9.

Turn the polenta out on a chopping board and cut into chips. Line a tray with non-stick baking parchment, brush with a little oil then arrange the chips in rows without them touching. Brush a little oil on the top of the chips and bake for 15 minutes then turn over and return to the oven for a further 10 minutes.

Season with an extra little shake of Himalayan salt before serving with fermented ketchup.

MAKI ROLLS

At first people tend to be intimidated by making sushi rolls, and it's true it's not easy to keep all the ingredients together. But, like most things, with loads of encouragement, practice and a few laughs, eventually you'll get the hang of it. Practise this with your mates and by the time it comes to serving maki rolls for a party, you'll be a pro.

Our maki rolls are made with quinoa instead of white rice to give a complete protein boost, and a mix of white, red and black quinoa looks great. Using quinoa does make it just that little bit harder to roll, but at least you will have good clean fun while practising. You need a sushi mat to make the rolls.

PREP	25 minutes if you are a beginner/ 5 minutes once you've mastered it
COOK	(quinoa) 15 minutes + cool time
MAKES	4 rolls/32 pieces

550g (1lb 3oz) cooked
  quinoa
1 teaspoon wasabi powder
1 small bunch of coriander
  leaves, chopped
3 tablespoons toasted
  sesame seeds
4 organic toasted
  nori sheets
8 chive lengths
1 ripe avocado, halved,
  stoned, peeled and sliced
4 large shiitake
  mushrooms, sliced and
  roasted in coconut oil
  until crisp
160g (5oz) enoki
  mushrooms
½ red pepper, thinly sliced
  into long strips
tamari sauce, for dipping

Mix the cooked quinoa, wasabi, coriander and sesame seeds in a bowl.

Take a sheet of nori and place it, shiny side face down, on the sushi mat.

Place a quarter of the quinoa mix on the nori sheet and use your fingers to spread the quinoa outwards right to the edge of both sides of the sheet and half way up.

Lay on a quarter of the chives with the ends protruding, avocado slices, shiitake mushrooms, enoki mushrooms with heads protruding at either end, and the red pepper slices.

Pick up the sushi mat with your thumbs and use it to roll the nori sheet over the ingredients while pushing back with your fingers. It's a bit like trying to roll a sleeping bag up tightly. You must keep the maki rolls compact and tight.

When it has come together, take the maki roll out of the mat and start another.

It's best to let the rolls rest for an hour in the fridge before serving.

Use a very sharp knife to cut each roll into 8 slices. Serve with tamari sauce.

WATERMELON CUPS

Many of our favourite celebrity chefs have done recipes for watermelon salads over the past decade and they are all amazingly delicious – IF, and only if, the watermelon is perfect. But how can you tell if it will be? First, weigh it up – it should be heavier than it looks. Second, look for its beauty spot – watermelons develop a mark where they rest on the ground, and a true beauty will sport a creamy yellow one. Third, give it a slap and a tap – a Bobby Dazzler of a melon will resonate with a deep hollow sound, whereas a lesser one will sound simply dull.

If you are not a good judge of character, you can always play it safe and buy your watermelon by the piece.

PREP	15 minutes + melon choosing time
MAKES	party canapés for 20

about 1.5kg (3lb 5oz) watermelon (unpeeled weight)
250g (9oz) shop-bought vegan 'cream cheese'
cold-pressed olive oil infused with lemon, for drizzling
50g (1¾oz) roasted pecans, chopped into crumbs
5 pitted black Kalamata olives, quartered
20 small fresh mint tips
cracked black pepper

Remove the rind and any pips from the watermelon, and cut into 3–4cm perfect cubes (keep the offcuts to juice or eat later).

Using a small melon baller, scoop out a cavity deep enough to pipe the 'cream cheese' in, being careful not to go through the base.

We like to pipe the cream cheese in using a small fluted nozzle, but you can just spoon it in.

At this point you can store the watermelon cups in the fridge for a few hours and finish later.

Pour a thin drizzle of late harvest lemon oil on the cheese and sprinkle with the pecan crumb and cracked black pepper.

Place a quartered Kalamata olive, shiny side up, on top. Spike with mint tips and serve.

CHARGRILLED
COURGETTE ROLL UPS

Macadamias are native to Australia and are a rich source of vitamin A, iron, protein, thiamin, riboflavin, niacin and folates as well as zinc, copper, calcium, phosphorus, potassium, magnesium and selenium. Wow, what a powerhouse of nutrition! After munching on these gorgeous energy-enriched canapés your guests will be bouncing around the party. As well as being madly nutritious and tasty, these roll ups are so pretty, although it might take you a few goes to get right. The macadamia cheese needs to be thick enough to hold the roll together, the filling must poke out of the top but not protrude from the bottom. (No one wants a protruding bottom. Unless you are having *that* sort of a party.)

PREP	30 minutes
SOAK	4 hours
SERVES	20

4 courgettes
Himalayan salt
20 fresh large mint leaves
20 basil leaves
40 wild rocket fronds
  (less than a bag)
2 long red chillies,

To make the cream cheese, drain the macadamia nuts and rinse thoroughly. Tip all the ingredients except the chives into a food processor and blitz until smooth. Mix in the chives and refrigerate until required. The cheese will last, chilled, for 3–4 days.

Now wash, dry and trim the ends off each courgette. Slice into long thin strips – the best way to achieve this is to slice on a mandolin or Japanese vegetable slicer.

deseeded and sliced
very thinly lengthways
(julienned)

FOR THE CREAM CHEESE
65g (2¼oz) macadamia
nuts, soaked in cold
water for 2–4 hours
1 tablespoon nutritional
yeast
zest of ¼ lemon
1 tablespoon fresh lemon
juice
½ tablespoon chopped
chives
pinch of Himalayan salt

Season the strips with a little Himalayan salt
and then dry fry in a very hot frying pan for
30 seconds each side. The pan should be
really quite hot so the strips get some colour
and become pliable without cooking through
completely.

Lay the courgette strips out to cool on kitchen
paper to absorb the excess liquid.

Transfer the strips to a clean chopping board
and spread a little macadamia cream cheese end
to end – allow about a generous teaspoonful.

Place one mint leaf, one basil leaf, a couple
of fronds of rocket and a julienned slice of chilli
on top of the cream cheese, spacing them out
along the courgette strip with the filling poking
out of the top. Roll up from the smaller end first.

Set the roll ups upright with herbs and fronds
cascading from the top. Chill, uncovered, until
required. Eat within a few hours, as the leaves
will start to droop.

MISO GLAZED BABY AUBERGINE SKEWERS

We are giving away one of our most precious secrets with this miraculous recipe, combining Japanese and Middle Eastern inspiration to create something truly magical. This dish is one of our most popular menu items, particularly for non-vegans – it's so unctuous and meaty, it's really hard to believe it's actually vegan! Just be prepared for the lull in conversation when you serve these as everyone sighs with pleasure.

PREP	10 minutes
COOK	30 minutes
MAKES	20

8 Japanese or baby
  aubergines
1 teaspoon Himalayan salt
25g (1oz) toasted sesame
  seeds

FOR THE GLAZE
150g (5½oz) white miso
300ml (½ pint) mirin
50g (1¾oz) coconut sugar
50g (1¾oz) fresh ginger,
  peeled and grated
150ml (¼ pint) sesame oil

FOR THE TAHINI DRESSING
1 garlic clove, crushed
50ml (2fl oz) cold water
50ml (2fl oz) freshly
  squeezed lemon juice
75ml (2½fl oz) tahini
½ teaspoon Himalayan salt

TO SERVE
pomegranate seeds
50g (1¾oz) toasted pine
  nuts
micro basil, if possible,
  or shredded basil leaves

Preheat the oven to 240°C/475°F/gas mark 9 and line a baking tray with greaseproof paper.

Prepare the aubergines by cutting into 2.5cm (1-in) thick rounds. Place in a single layer on the lined tray and season with Himalayan salt. Transfer to the oven and roast until golden brown and cooked through, about 20 minutes, then cool on the tray.

Meanwhile prepare the glaze. Blitz all the glaze ingredients in a blender, then pour into a small saucepan and bring to the boil for a few minutes, stirring all the while.

To make the tahini dressing, place all the ingredients in a bowl and whisk until thickened.

To assemble, skewer the aubergines, apply the glaze generously using a pastry brush and sprinkle on the toasted sesame seeds.

Reheat the aubergines in the oven until sticky and caramelised – about 10 minutes.

Serve on a platter with a drizzle of tahini dressing, pomegranate seeds, pine nuts and micro basil.

BLISS BALLS

Bliss balls are by far the best-selling sweet treats in our restaurants, although that might be partly down to the giggling we get when people ask for them. These truffles are so rich and indulgent that you would think they must be sinful. Have no fear or guilt! Luckily they are loaded with antioxidants, vitamins and minerals so it's a true case of 'spoil yourself without spoiling yourself'. Expect gasps, groans and a round of applause from your guests. One important request: make sure you use the pulse button on your food processor when making the truffle mixture because it is hard work for the machine. For making sugar-free, wheat-free and vegan desserts your food processor is your most important piece of kit and needs to be loved and cared for, like a middle aged man with his classic car.

PREP	30 minutes
SOAK	60 minutes
CHILL	60 minutes
MAKES	20 truffles

375g (13¼oz) pitted
  Medjool dates
180ml (6fl oz) raw cold-
  pressed coconut oil,
  melted
100g (3½oz) unsweetened
  raw cacao powder
1 teaspoon vanilla essence
½ teaspoon Himalayan salt
125ml (4fl oz) almond milk
100g (3½oz) dried
  desiccated coconut, for
  coating

Soak the dates in pre-boiled and cooled water for at least an hour, then drain. (We worked out recently that this helps to prevent burning out the motor of your food processor.)

Put the melted coconut oil, drained dates, cacao, vanilla essence and Himalayan salt in a food processor. (Again, we implore everyone, in the restaurant and at home, to use the food processor on the PULSE mode rather than continuously running; even presoaking the dates won't protect the motor of your food processor from burnout if you leave it running.)

Pour the almond milk into the date mix while pulsing until the truffle mix looks completely smooth.

Scrape the mixture into a bowl then cover and place in the fridge overnight or in the freezer for an hour to firm up. Roll into bite-sized balls using your hands, which is a sticky business...

Have the coconut ready in a tray and drop in each truffle then shake the tray to coat the truffles evenly. The balls of bliss will last in the fridge for at least a week or in the freezer for months.

INDEX

GRATITUDES

An enormous thanks to Tara O Sullivan from Kyle Books, who convinced us to write the book in the first place. We are so grateful not only for her skill as editor but for her democratic guidance, infinite patience and good-natured way of nudging us along to the finish line.

One of the many joys of working on this book was witnessing the magic happen on set, so a huge thanks to the lovely prop stylist Agathe Gits for her wonderful eye for choosing props to best showcase our the 'spoil yourself without spoiling yourself' lifestyle. The look of this book owes much to the genius of Catherine Gratwicke for her stunning photography with such amazing richness and depth. She did more than capture the image, she bought everything to life. And many thanks to Evi O for laying out the book in such a classy fashion.

Bucket loads of love to our friend and business partner Lisa Inglis for holding the Redemption reins whilst we created, tested and spent long stretches of time at the computer.

Massive thank you to Sara Halbard for believing in Redemption from the early days and helping us to get to this point.

Thank you to all of the Redemption family past and present, for joining us on this incredible journey - you are all a big part of this book coming together. And thank you to our barman Kyran O'Donoghue for letting us shoot his beautiful vagabond hands.

CATHERINE I'm very grateful to my family and friends who have given so much support and advice to me and the Redemption project and particularly to Damian Schnabel for his wonderful work with the brand logo and mandalas.

ANDREA It's not what we have in our life but who we have in our life that counts, so much love and gratitude goes out to all my family, especially to my children Joe and Lucy for teaching me to be a better human and for being gracious enough not to comment on how much I work.

I am truly grateful to James for being my sounding board, my safety net and the most unwavering advocate of Redemption.

Love and peas,

Andrea and Catherine xx